SpringerBriefs in Information Systems

Series Editor

Jörg Becker, Münster, Germany

SpringerBriefs present concise summaries of cutting-edge research and practical applications across a wide spectrum of fields. Featuring compact volumes of 50 to 125 pages, the series covers a range of content from professional to academic. Typical topics might include: A timely report of state-of-the art analytical techniques, a bridge between new research results, as published in journal articles, and a contextual literature review, a snapshot of a hot or emerging topic, an in-depth case study or practical example, a presentation of core concepts that students must understand in order to make independent contributions. SpringerBriefs in Information Systems showcase emerging theory, empirical research, and practical application in all subcategories of information systems and related fields, from a global author community. Briefs are characterized by fast, global electronic dissemination, standard publishing contracts, standardized manuscript preparation and formatting guidelines, and expedited production schedules.

Isabel Ramos • Katrin Bergener • Armin Stein
Editors

Hybrid Attention in Organizations

How Artificial Intelligence Augments Learning, Decision-Making, and Human Intelligence

Springer

Editors
Isabel Ramos
Department of Information Systems
University of Minho
Guimarães, Portugal

Katrin Bergener
Department of Information Systems
University of Münster
Münster, Nordrhein-Westfalen, Germany

Armin Stein
Department of Information Systems
University of Münster
Münster, Nordrhein-Westfalen, Germany

ISSN 2192-4929 ISSN 2192-4937 (electronic)
SpringerBriefs in Information Systems
ISBN 978-3-032-30185-7 ISBN 978-3-032-30186-4 (eBook)
https://doi.org/10.1007/978-3-032-30186-4

This Springer imprint is published by the registered company Springer Nature Switzerland AG
The registered company address is: Gewerbestrasse 11, 6330 Cham, Switzerland

Preface: From Human to Hybrid Attention: Generative AI and the Future of Organizational Sensemaking

Generative artificial intelligence (GenAI) is transforming how organizations make decisions and construct meaning from data. Modern transformer-based models rely on *attention mechanisms* that enable AI to focus on salient information—an innovation that has become the foundation of contemporary generative systems. Within organizations, these mechanisms act as cognitive infrastructures that filter, prioritize, and contextualize knowledge. By transforming data into feedback-driven learning loops, they link computational processes to higher-level organizational sensemaking.

This volume examines the transition from *human* to *hybrid attention*, where human and machine focus intertwine in complex environments. GenAI thus extends the boundaries of knowledge-intensive work by combining human interpretation with algorithmic precision. The book results from systematic literature reviews conducted by students of the research seminar *AI and Attention in the Organization*, offered in Summer Term 2025 within the Bachelor of Science in Information Systems Program at the Department of Information Systems, University of Münster, Germany. The seminar explored how emerging forms of artificial and human attention jointly shape organizational learning and decision-making in the age of GenAI.

Three interrelated themes structure the volume. The first concerns *human-centered AI design* for *intelligence augmentation*. It shows that AI can amplify rather than replace human cognition when systems are aligned with human interpretive capacities, incorporate structured oversight, and embed ethical values such as transparency and fairness. The second theme addresses *AI-augmented attention in decision-making*, explaining how AI enhances decision quality and timeliness by filtering complex data while humans contribute contextual judgment, intuition, and ethical discernment. The third examines *AI attention in organizational learning*, illustrating how attention-based systems convert feedback into reflexive cycles of knowledge refinement and collective understanding. Together, these perspectives depict a shift from automation to augmentation, one that strengthens human creativity, judgment, and organizational intelligence.

Several cross-cutting issues connect these inquiries. Foremost is the design of *human–AI collaboration*, which seeks balance between automation and augmentation. Effective hybrid systems combine machine scalability and analytical depth with human sensemaking and creativity. *Trust and interpretability* emerge as central conditions for such collaboration: users must understand and appropriately trust AI outputs, which requires transparency, explainability, and human oversight mechanisms. *Ethical design* also permeates the discussion, emphasizing fairness, accountability, and human agency as core design constraints rather than afterthoughts. These principles embody a socio-technical view, where the success of hybrid attention depends not only on algorithmic innovation but also on how humans use, interpret, and govern these systems.

This book is intended for researchers and graduate students in Information Systems, Organizational Studies, and Human–AI Interaction. Synthesizing interdisciplinary evidence, it offers conceptual and practical insights into how GenAI reshapes organizational knowledge and action. More broadly, it contributes to advancing theory and practice by integrating fragmented debates into a coherent understanding of *hybrid attention*. The chapters demonstrate that when human artificial intelligence and artificial intelligence are designed to complement each other, organizations can learn and decide more intelligently, thus retaining human judgment and values at the center of technological progress. We hope this volume will inspire scholars, students, and practitioners to envision organizational sensemaking powered by the synergy of human and AI attention.

Guimaraes, Portugal — Isabel Ramos
Münster, Germany — Katrin Bergener
Münster, Germany — Armin Stein

Contents

Foundations: Attention and Intelligence in Organizations

AI Attention Mechanisms Enhancing Organisational Learning: A Systematic Literature Review

Jan Hermann Ernst, Nils Waltering, and Isabel Ramos

Declarations

- ChatGPT was used to improve the final quality of the text. ChatGPT was also used to identify the initial search strings for the articles to be included in the first phase of the literature review. The authors later refined these initial strings through successive adjustments and verification of the results. The authors reviewed and take full responsibility for the content of this chapter.

1 Introduction

The ability to acquire, share, and apply knowledge has become a decisive driver of organisational success. As firms operate in increasingly complex and dynamic environments, knowledge has shifted from a supporting function to a strategic asset essential for innovation and sustained competitive advantage. Rooted in the knowledge-based view of the firm, this perspective posits that knowledge constitutes a unique, hard-to-replicate resource that enables the development of distinctive organisational capabilities (Tsoi & Strønen, 2024; Alavi et al., 2024).

Recent advances in artificial intelligence (AI) have opened new possibilities for enhancing knowledge management (KM) processes, introducing mechanisms capable of supporting how organisations capture feedback, generate insights, and learn. Among these advances, AI attention mechanisms enable systems to selectively focus on the most relevant information. These mechanisms have emerged as particularly promising tools for improving the precision and adaptability of knowledge processes. Scholars have highlighted AI's potential to augment all core KM functions, including knowledge acquisition, storage, sharing, and application (Jarrahi et al., 2023a, 2023b; Alavi et al., 2024). As Jarrahi et al. (2023a) note, the diffusion

J. H. Ernst · N. Waltering
Department of Information Systems, University of Münster, Münster, Germany
e-mail: jan.ernst@uni-muenster.de; nils.waltering@uni-muenster.de

I. Ramos (✉)
Department of Information Systems, University of Minho, Guimarães, Portugal
e-mail: iramos@dsi.uminho.pt

I. Ramos et al. (eds.), *Hybrid Attention in Organizations*, SpringerBriefs in Information Systems, https://doi.org/10.1007/978-3-032-30186-4_1

of AI capabilities is expected to permeate nearly all organisational activities. Yet, despite the growing acknowledgement of AI's transformative role, its specific functional contribution to organisational learning remains underexplored (Jo & Park, 2024).

In particular, limited research has examined how AI attention mechanisms influence learning outcomes when relevance itself may be biased or context-dependent (Jo & Park, 2024). Prior studies have largely emphasised AI's potential (particularly GenAI systems) benefits rather than empirically investigating its integration with organisational learning routines and feedback processes, especially in dynamic contexts where traditional KM systems struggle to adapt to evolving knowledge needs (Alavi et al., 2024; Budhwar et al., 2022; Leoni et al., 2024). Moreover, recent literature has begun to expose the potential unintended consequences of GenAI in KM, including reduced human collaboration, reinforcement of existing knowledge biases, and over-reliance on algorithmic outputs (Retkowsky et al., 2024). These issues compound long-standing challenges organisations face in managing knowledge effectively amid information overload, fragmented expertise, and weak feedback loops (Alavi et al., 2024).

Against this backdrop, AI attention mechanisms offer a novel means to address these challenges by filtering, prioritising, and aligning knowledge flows with organisational learning goals (Jarrahi et al., 2023a). Understanding how these mechanisms operate within learning and feedback processes is therefore essential to ensure that GenAI complements human cognition and collaboration in knowledge creation.

Accordingly, the aim of this systematic literature review (SLR) is to investigate how AI attention mechanisms enhance organisational learning, particularly through feedback processes that facilitate knowledge acquisition and sharing. The following research question guides it:

How do AI attention mechanisms support organisational learning by enhancing knowledge acquisition and sharing through feedback processes?

Using the SPICE framework, this review systematically examines evidence from interdisciplinary organisational studies to:

1. Clarify how AI attention mechanisms support feedback-driven learning processes;
2. Identify enablers and barriers affecting AI-assisted knowledge management; and
3. Reveal conceptual and empirical blind spots that constrain current understanding.

The review contributes to both theory and practice by offering a clearer picture of how AI systems interact with human learning processes to promote sustainable and adaptive knowledge practices. It establishes a conceptual foundation for future empirical studies and theoretical developments aiming to integrate AI attention mechanisms into organisational strategies.

This chapter is structured as follows. Section 2 provides an overview of relevant topics. Section 3 outlines the SLR methodology and its limitations. Section 4 presents the main findings, distinguishing between general trends and content-specific insights relevant to the research question. Section 5 discusses theoretical implications, research gaps, and practical considerations, and Section 6 concludes with final remarks and directions for future research.

2 Conceptual Foundations of AI Attention in Organisational Learning

This section provides an overview of the conceptual foundations underpinning this study and establishes a shared understanding of the main topics addressed. It introduces the principles of AI attention mechanisms, outlines their relevance for organisational learning, and connects them to knowledge management and feedback processes that together frame the scope of this review.

2.1 AI Attention Mechanisms

Attention mechanisms are a core technique in modern machine learning that enable neural networks to selectively focus on the most relevant parts of input data. By assigning weights that express the relative importance of each element in a sequence, attention mechanisms enhance a model's capacity to capture contextual dependencies and relationships between data points. This innovation underlies the *transformer architecture*, which has become the foundation of the current generation of generative AI models (Bergmann & Stryker, 2024).

In organisational contexts, attention mechanisms offer capabilities beyond computational efficiency. They enable systems to identify, prioritise, and relate knowledge in ways that can directly support learning processes (Jarrahi et al., 2023a). By dynamically emphasising relevant inputs, they can strengthen both knowledge acquisition and knowledge sharing, particularly through more focused and adaptive feedback loops (Mancuso et al., 2025).

This review, therefore, includes only papers focusing on AI systems that explicitly or implicitly implement attention mechanisms. Accordingly, the terms *artificial intelligence*, *AI*, and *generative AI (GenAI)* are used interchangeably to refer to systems that incorporate such mechanisms. The analysis adopts a functional perspective, emphasising how these systems operate within knowledge processes rather than detailing their technical architecture. While acknowledging the technical underpinnings of transformer models, the chapter concentrates on their organisational implications. Specifically, the chapter focuses on how attention-based AI contributes to knowledge-related learning outcomes.

2.2 *Organisational Context and Learning*

The organisational context can be defined as the situational opportunities and constraints that shape behaviour and determine the meaning and effectiveness of organisational activities (Johns, 2006). It represents the environment in which shared goals are pursued and collective knowledge is generated. This review focuses on studies situated within such defined contexts, ensuring that findings are grounded in real organisational dynamics.

Organisational learning is understood as a dynamic, collective process through which members share experiences and knowledge to develop new competencies and adapt to changing environments (Tetrick & Camburn, 2004). It strengthens both individual and collective capabilities, enhances innovation and responsiveness to competitive pressures, and supports organisational resilience (Olan et al., 2022; Ritala et al., 2024).

Understanding these foundational concepts is essential for analysing how knowledge-related processes unfold in digitally transformed environments. GenAI systems operate within and reshape these contexts by influencing how information is filtered, interpreted, and distributed across organisational actors.

2.3 *Knowledge Management*

KM provides the structural and cultural foundation for organisational learning. Alavi and Leidner (1999) define knowledge as a *justified personal belief that increases an individual's capacity to take effective action*, emphasising that knowledge ultimately resides in people rather than in information repositories. KM is thus a systematic, organisation-specific process for acquiring, organising, and communicating both tacit and explicit knowledge.

Knowledge acquisition involves capturing and integrating knowledge within the organisation, whereas knowledge sharing refers to the *pull* of information by individuals rather than a purely technological *push* (Alavi & Leidner, 1999). Successful KM requires alignment among cultural, managerial, and technological dimensions. Recent accounts of AI-enabled knowledge management suggest that AI marks a new generation in the evolution of KM, extending earlier technological approaches toward more intelligent and adaptive knowledge processes (Bencsik, 2021).

A key theoretical foundation is Nonaka's SECI model (Nonaka, 1994), which explains how organisational knowledge is dynamically created through continuous interaction between *tacit* (personal, experiential) and *explicit* (codified) forms of knowledge. The four conversion processes, namely socialisation, externalisation, combination, and internalisation, describe how individual knowledge becomes organisational knowledge.

This model is highly relevant to the present study because it illustrates how feedback and knowledge-sharing mechanisms foster learning. In particular, the externalisation and internalisation stages reveal opportunities for AI attention mechanisms to transform individual insights into shared organisational knowledge. Most of the reviewed studies build conceptually on these foundational perspectives, providing a lens for analysing how attention-based AI systems can support knowledge-related learning processes.

2.4 *Feedback Processes*

In this chapter, feedback processes are conceptualised as interactive mechanisms through which knowledge is validated, refined, and adapted in response to user input and contextual needs (Mancuso et al., 2025). Feedback acts as a connective tissue between knowledge acquisition and knowledge sharing, facilitating both individual and collective learning (Alavi et al., 2024).

In AI-supported environments, feedback loops are not merely reactive but serve as drivers of continuous adaptation and personalisation. GenAI systems, for example, iteratively adjust their outputs in response to user prompts, enabling mutual refinement and contextual alignment. Through these interactions, feedback becomes a process of *co-learning* between humans and AI systems, contributing to the emergence of adaptive and context-aware organisational learning (Kostis et al., 2024; Mancuso et al., 2025).

This theoretical framing positions AI attention mechanisms as enablers of organisational learning, linking technical innovation to cognitive and social processes within firms. By integrating insights from organisational learning theory, KM models, and feedback dynamics, it establishes the conceptual foundation for the systematic literature review presented in the following section.

3 Structured Review Methodology Using the SPICE Framework

This section outlines the methodological approach adopted in this SLR. To ensure rigour, transparency, and replicability, the review followed the structured literature review guidelines proposed by vom Brocke et al. (2015). The research design was guided by the SPICE framework, which offers a robust approach for defining the scope and parameters of qualitative reviews. Compared to quantitative-oriented frameworks such as PICO, SPICE provides greater flexibility for capturing complex, context-sensitive evidence across organisational and technological domains.

3.1 *Application of the SPICE Framework*

The SPICE framework was applied to ensure conceptual clarity and methodological consistency throughout the review. Each element is detailed below.

Setting The study focuses on organisational environments as the primary empirical setting. These contexts provide the structural, cultural, and procedural conditions that influence how knowledge is created, shared, and retained. This focus ensures that the analysis reflects authentic organisational dynamics in which AI attention mechanisms operate, thereby increasing ecological validity.

Perspective The review adopts a multi-level attentional perspective encompassing: (a) human attention—how individuals focus and filter information; (b) AI attention—how artificial systems identify and prioritise information; and (c) organisational attention—how collectives allocate cognitive and informational resources. This integrative lens enables an examination of how human and machine attention interact and co-evolve, rather than being treated as isolated phenomena.

Intervention The intervention under investigation concerns the implementation of AI attention mechanisms designed to enhance organisational learning. These mechanisms perform filtering, prioritisation, and focusing functions that influence knowledge acquisition and sharing within organisational settings.

Comparison The review contrasts organisations that adopt AI attention mechanisms with those that rely on traditional knowledge management systems. This comparison clarifies whether AI primarily acts as a substitute or an augmenter of human and organisational learning processes.

Evaluation Evaluation criteria focus on how AI attention mechanisms contribute to organisational learning effectiveness. Specific indicators include improvements in knowledge acquisition and sharing, reduced information overload, strengthened feedback loops, and mitigation of cognitive bottlenecks. Potential adverse effects, such as attentional fragmentation or over-reliance on algorithmic filtering, were also considered.

3.2 Search Strategy

A comprehensive search strategy was developed by operationalising the SPICE elements into precise search terms and controlled vocabularies. Synonyms and wildcard operators were employed to capture linguistic variations (e.g., "*information filtering*", "*knowledge prioritization*", "*attention model*").

Table 1 presents the final search string applied in Scopus, ensuring reproducibility of the search process

Table 1 Final search string

Source	Final Search String
Scopus	TITLE-ABS-KEY ((“organization*” OR “firm” OR “enterprise” OR “company”) AND (“AI” OR “artificial intelligence” OR “AI attention mechanism”) AND (“attention” OR “attention mechanism*” OR “transformer*” OR “human attention” OR “focus” OR “information filtering” OR “information prioritization” OR “decision-making” OR “innovation”) AND (“knowledge management” OR “knowledge acquisition” OR “knowledge sharing” OR “knowledge transfer” OR “knowledge creation” OR “knowledge dissemination” OR “feedback” OR “feedback processes” OR “feedback loop*” OR “learning process*”) AND (“organizational learning”) AND PUBYEAR > 2019 AND PUBYEAR < 2026 AND (LIMIT-TO (DOCTYPE, “ar”) OR LIMIT-TO (DOCTYPE, “cp”)) AND (LIMIT-TO (LANGUAGE, “English”))

Table 2 Selected databases and retrieved papers

Database	Filter	Number of papers
Scopus	Peer-reviewed journal and conference papers (2020–2025, English)	56
AIS eLibrary	Conference proceedings (AIS family conferences)	1
ScienceDirect	Journal articles (2020–2025, English)	3

3.3 Searched Academic Databases

To ensure extensive and multidisciplinary coverage, three major academic databases were consulted (Table 2).

Scopus was prioritised for its breadth across IS, management, and computer-science domains. The AIS eLibrary was included to capture influential contributions from the Information Systems community, while ScienceDirect provided high-quality, peer-reviewed studies from management and technology journals. Journal rankings were verified through the SCImago Journal Rank (SJR) to ensure that only credible, peer-reviewed outlets were included.

3.4 Eligibility Criteria

To preserve methodological rigour, explicit inclusion and exclusion criteria were applied. First, only peer-reviewed journal articles and conference papers were considered to maintain academic quality and credibility. Second, publications had to appear in recognised, ranked outlets, verified through the SJR, thereby ensuring scholarly impact and reliability. Third, the publication period was restricted to 2020–2025 to capture the most recent developments in AI attention mechanisms and organisational learning. Fourth, all studies had to be written in English and accessible in full text, allowing for comprehensive analysis of methods, findings, and theoretical framing. Finally, inclusion required a clear conceptual or empirical connection between AI attention mechanisms, organisational learning, and feedback-driven knowledge processes. Collectively, these criteria ensured that only contemporary, high-quality research directly relevant to the study's focus was included in the review.

Studies were excluded from the review when they did not meet the established quality or relevance thresholds. Specifically, non-peer-reviewed materials, such as editorials, book chapters, reports, preprints, or theses, were removed to maintain methodological rigour. Publications were also excluded when they fell outside the temporal scope (i.e., published before 2020), were not written in English, or lacked full-text accessibility.

Furthermore, studies unrelated to organisational contexts were excluded, including those focused solely on technical or algorithmic aspects of AI without examining human or organisational implications. Similarly, individual-level analyses that did not address collective learning, knowledge management, or feedback processes within organisations were omitted. Finally, papers with insufficient empirical or conceptual relevance were excluded. Examples of excluded studies were those addressing general AI topics without explicit reference to attention mechanisms or organisational learning.

Together, these exclusions ensured that the final corpus of studies represented credible, contemporary, and contextually relevant contributions to understanding how AI attention mechanisms support organisational learning.

3.5 Study-Selection Process

As shown in Fig. 1, the initial search process yielded a total of 60 records. After removing duplicates and non-academic materials, 27 papers remained. A forward and backward citation search identified 25 additional sources, yielding a total of 52 studies. Screening of titles and abstracts excluded 24 irrelevant papers, and 13 additional studies were removed following full-text review. The final corpus comprised *15 primary studies*, which formed the empirical basis for analysis.

This multi-stage selection process adheres to best-practice standards for systematic reviews, ensuring both transparency and reproducibility.

3.6 Data Extraction and Analysis

All data were extracted into a structured *Notion* database, which facilitated systematic organisation and cross-referencing of study characteristics. For each paper, the following elements were recorded:

- Bibliographic information (authors, year, source, citations).
- Methodological details (design, data collection, context).
- Analytical focus (knowledge acquisition, sharing, or feedback processes).

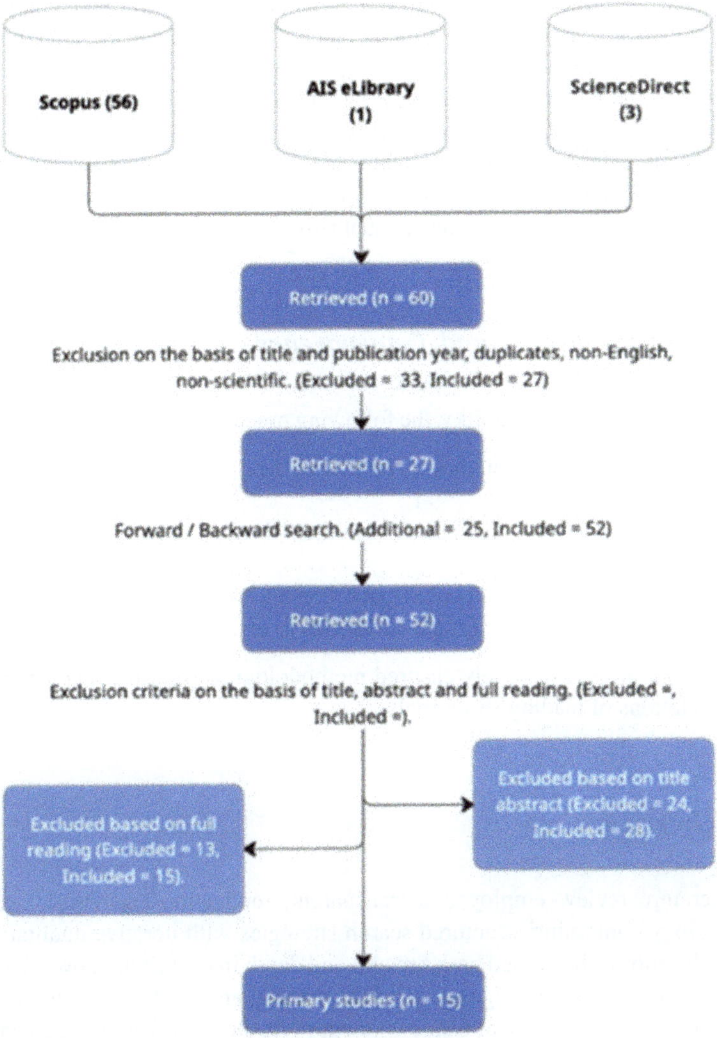

Fig. 1 Study-selection process

The data were then exported to Microsoft Excel for coding and synthesis. An inductive thematic analysis was applied to identify recurrent patterns, methodological trends, and conceptual linkages across studies.

During the initial coding phase, emergent themes revealed overlapping interpretations of "knowledge acquisition" and "knowledge sharing". A second round of full-text coding was therefore performed to refine categorisations and capture more nuanced insights into feedback-driven learning processes. This iterative approach aligns with the interpretive rigour recommended in qualitative IS research (Myers & Klein, 2011).

3.7 *Ensuring Rigour and Transparency*

To enhance validity and reliability, the following procedural safeguards were applied:

1. Comprehensive documentation of search strings, database filters, and selection decisions.
2. Triangulation through the use of multiple databases and backward/forward searches.
3. Auditability supported by detailed extraction logs stored in the Notion workspace.
4. Iterative refinement of analytical categories to ensure conceptual saturation.

These measures collectively ensured methodological robustness consistent with the expectations of leading IS journals.

3.8 *Overview*

The literature review employed a transparent, replicable, and context-sensitive methodology combining structured search strategies with iterative qualitative synthesis. The approach enabled both breadth and depth in examining how AI attention mechanisms shape knowledge acquisition, sharing, and feedback within organisations. The resulting analytical framework supports the empirical findings and theoretical contributions presented in the subsequent sections.

4 Synthesised Findings on AI Attention Mechanisms in Organisational Learning

This section presents the results of the literature review based on the 15 studies that met all inclusion criteria. The findings are organised into seven subsections, progressing from a descriptive overview of the reviewed works to their conceptual, operational, and organisational implications. The section concludes with a synthesis of cross-cutting themes and a summary of the main insights derived from the corpus.

4.1 Descriptive Overview of the Selected Studies

As shown in Fig. 2, a pronounced increase in publication activity since 2023, peaking in 2024. This trend parallels the surge in GenAI adoption within organisational settings. The rapid growth signals a shift in scholarly focus towards understanding AI attention mechanisms as integral components of knowledge and learning processes.

As shown in Fig. 3, qualitative research designs dominate the field, representing 87% of all studies. Quantitative approaches remain rare, reflecting the exploratory stage of this research domain.

Table 3 summarises the distribution of research objectives. Most studies (53%) sought to empirically test or illustrate conceptual frameworks; one-third (33%) developed practical tools or guidelines; 13% proposed theoretical extensions; and one study (7%) focused on methodological guidance.

4.2 Thematic Structure of the Literature

As displayed in Fig. 4, the themes identified in the reviewed studies reveal that Human–AI collaboration appears most prominently, followed by applications for AI, GenAI, and GenA-driven decision-making, with the remaining themes (e.g. AI tools, risks and benefits, explainability, innovation, learning and education) occurring less frequently and forming a long tail of more specialised concerns.

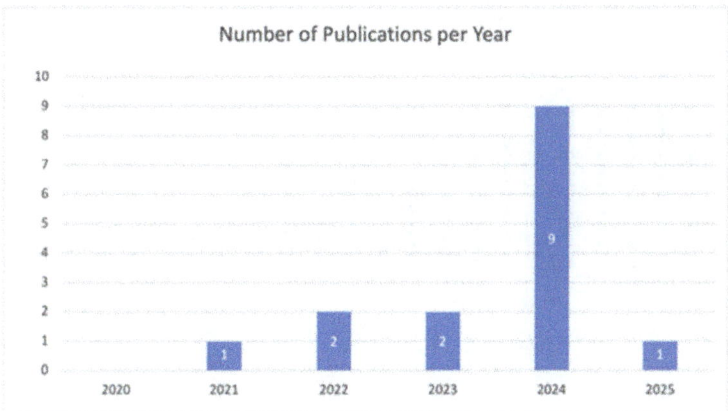

Fig. 2 Increase in publication counts from 2023 to 2024

Fig. 3 Qualitative vs. Quantitative studies

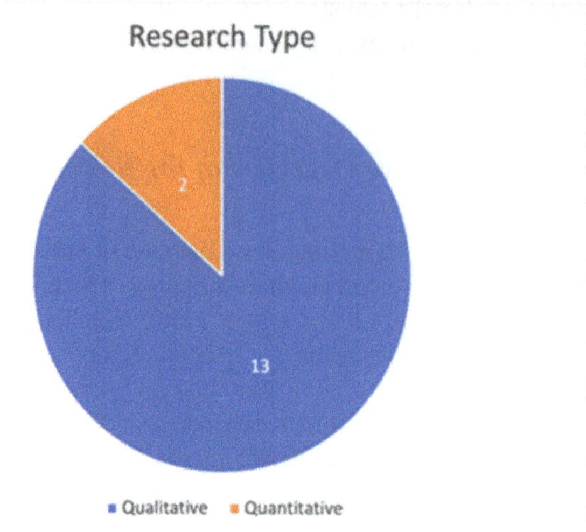

Table 3 Distribution of research objectives among included studies

Research objective	Description	Share of studies (%)
Empirical explanation and validation	Test or demonstrate theoretical propositions using real-world data	53
Framework development	Propose structured approaches or models for applying AI in learning	33
Theoretical model construction	Introduce new conceptualisations of AI attention and learning	13
Methodological contribution	Offer guidance for research design or assessment	7

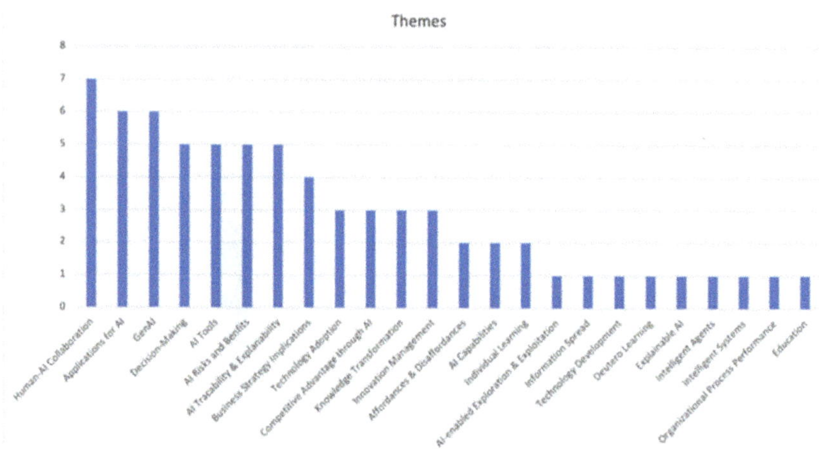

Fig. 4 Distribution of thematic categories identified across the reviewed studies

A detailed analysis of the themes in the figure allowed for outlining a key thematic structure to organise the themes into interrelated clusters around Human–AI collaboration, Generative AI, strategic and performance outcomes, and trust, traceability, and explainability issues.

The analysis of the reviewed studies reveals five dominant themes reflecting how artificial intelligence (AI) is being conceptualised and applied within organisational and cognitive contexts.

The first theme, *Human–AI collaboration*, centres on the interaction between human cognition and AI in knowledge-intensive work. Research in this stream explores how hybrid configurations of humans and intelligent systems enhance decision-making, creativity, and problem-solving, giving rise to notions such as *augmented cognition* and *hybrid teams*. These studies emphasise complementarity rather than substitution, highlighting how AI can extend human attentional and analytical capacities.

The second theme, *AI in organisational learning*, focuses on the adoption of AI tools to support knowledge acquisition, retention, and sharing. Scholars in this area examine how GenAI systems facilitate *learning enhancement* and *adaptive knowledge processes*, enabling organisations to capture tacit expertise, personalise learning experiences, and create more responsive knowledge ecosystems (Kaczorowska-Spychalska et al., 2024).

A third theme, *Generative AI*, addresses the growing role of large language models (LLMs) in creative and feedback-oriented tasks (Ramaul et al., 2024). This stream includes studies on *ChatGPT* and related tools, showing how generative models contribute to *co-creation*, content generation, and *automation* of cognitive tasks (Sumbal et al., 2024). Research in this domain explores both the productivity gains and the reconfiguration of human roles associated with AI-supported creativity.

The fourth theme, *strategic and performance outcomes*, examines the organisational and innovation benefits derived from AI adoption. These studies link the integration of intelligent systems with improvements in *efficiency*, *innovation capacity*, and *decision quality*, framing AI as a driver of competitive advantage and organisational transformation.

Finally, the fifth theme, *trust, traceability, and explainability*, concerns the *ethical and governance dimensions* of AI use. This body of work discusses how *transparency*, *accountability*, and the ability to explain AI decisions are critical to fostering user trust and ensuring responsible implementation.

Collectively, these five themes provide an integrated view of how AI technologies are reshaping cognition, learning, creativity, performance, and governance within organisations.

4.3 Conceptualisation of Attention Mechanisms

Across the reviewed literature, AI attention mechanisms are consistently portrayed as algorithmic structures inspired by human cognitive processes of selective focus. These mechanisms assign relative weights to different inputs, enabling systems to identify the most relevant information and capture contextual interdependencies within complex data streams (Bergmann & Stryker, 2024).

Two complementary perspectives emerge. The *functional perspective* views attention mechanisms primarily as computational tools that improve the precision and contextual accuracy of AI outputs. In this view, attention serves as a technical analogue to human selective attention, enhancing efficiency in data processing and retrieval. The *socio-technical perspective*, by contrast, interprets attention as a relational process that mediates collaboration between humans and machines. Here, attention mechanisms are not merely technical components but organisational mediators that shape collective sensemaking and knowledge exchange.

Together, these perspectives extend the concept of attention from an algorithmic principle to an organisational construct. They suggest that attention mechanisms act simultaneously as computational enablers and as cognitive interfaces that reshape how individuals and organisations perceive, interpret, and apply knowledge.

4.4 Operationalisation in AI Systems

Operationally, attention mechanisms are embedded most prominently within transformer architectures that underpin modern large language models and other GenAI systems. These architectures dynamically distribute focus across tokens or data elements, allowing models to derive meaning from contextual relationships and generate adaptive responses.

Within organisational applications, attention mechanisms typically function in three interrelated ways. First, they support knowledge integration and retrieval by consolidating information from disparate repositories and mitigating fragmentation across departments or systems. Second, they facilitate pattern recognition and insight generation, uncovering latent relationships in data that inform decision-making and innovation (Haefner et al., 2021; Jarrahi et al., 2023a). Finally, they enable personalised feedback loops, continuously refining outputs in response to user interaction and organisational context (Mancuso et al., 2025).

Through these operational modes, AI attention systems evolve into adaptive learning partners that continually improve their relevance and performance. They not only automate information processing but also contribute to ongoing organisational learning by refining how knowledge is accessed, interpreted, and applied.

4.5 Organisational Implications and Outcomes

The reviewed studies converge on the finding that AI attention mechanisms have a profound influence on knowledge-related processes within organisations. They enhance knowledge acquisition by enabling the integration of heterogeneous data sources, promoting continuous learning, and revealing tacit patterns that might otherwise remain unnoticed (Alavi et al., 2024). They also strengthen knowledge sharing, facilitating more transparent and inclusive access to information while bridging gaps between hierarchical or functional units.

At the same time, scholars highlight potential drawbacks. Over-reliance on algorithmic filtering can introduce biases and limit critical interpretation. The automation of cognitive tasks may lead to deskilling or reduced human engagement in reflective thinking (Retkowsky et al., 2024). Moreover, while attention mechanisms accelerate knowledge flows, they may inadvertently diminish interpersonal collaboration or informal knowledge exchange.

The literature thus portrays a dual dynamic: attention-based AI systems significantly expand organisational learning capacity but require deliberate governance to ensure human oversight, safeguard interpretive diversity, and sustain the social dimensions of learning.

4.6 Cross-Theme Analysis and Emerging Trends

A synthesis across themes reveals four major trends shaping the evolution of research in this field. First, there is a conceptual shift from automation to augmentation, as scholars increasingly describe AI attention mechanisms as tools that complement rather than replace human cognition (Wijnhoven, 2022). Future work is therefore urged to identify the boundary conditions under which human–AI complementarity yields optimal learning outcomes.

Second, feedback loops are emerging as central mechanisms linking AI performance with human learning. The literature emphasises that organisational learning benefits most when feedback between humans and AI is continuous, adaptive, and bidirectional, allowing systems to align dynamically with changing goals.

Third, studies are beginning to describe hybrid attention ecosystems, in which human, algorithmic, and material elements jointly shape attentional focus across organisational networks. This perspective introduces the idea of distributed or collective cognition, inviting further investigation into the socio-material foundations of organisational attention.

Finally, the field shows signs of increasing empirical validation. While early work was largely conceptual, recent studies have begun to employ field research, experiments, and case analyses to test theoretical models (Leoni et al., 2024). This methodological diversification signals a maturing research domain moving towards stronger empirical grounding.

Together, these developments illustrate a field transitioning from conceptual exploration towards the systematic study of hybrid human–AI attentional dynamics and their implications for sustainable organisational learning.

4.7 *Overview of the Literature Review Findings*

The findings of this review demonstrate that AI attention mechanisms constitute a pivotal advancement in how organisations acquire, share, and apply knowledge. By selectively filtering and prioritising information, these mechanisms enable firms to navigate information abundance and focus collective learning efforts on contextually relevant knowledge. In doing so, they enhance both the efficiency and adaptability of knowledge processes, reinforcing the central role of feedback as a driver of organisational learning.

The synthesis of evidence shows that attention mechanisms serve a dual function. On one hand, they act as technical enablers, improving the precision, coherence, and contextualisation of knowledge management activities. On the other hand, they operate as organisational mediators, shaping human cognition, collaboration patterns, and decision-making routines. This dual role redefines the boundaries of learning by distributing attention between human actors and intelligent systems, producing new configurations of hybrid cognition.

Across studies, three consistent patterns emerge. First, organisations that successfully integrate attention-based AI exhibit greater responsiveness to environmental change, as these systems facilitate the continuous updating of knowledge repositories. Second, AI-driven feedback loops foster reflexive learning, enabling both humans and machines to iteratively adjust their interpretations and outputs. Third, effective adoption requires a balance between algorithmic efficiency and human judgement, since the quality of organisational learning depends as much on critical reflection as on technological precision.

Nonetheless, the findings also reveal persistent challenges. Unchecked reliance on automated attention may narrow organisational focus, amplifying bias or excluding alternative perspectives. Similarly, excessive dependence on AI-generated outputs risks diminishing human analytical capabilities and collaborative dialogue. The literature therefore converges on a central proposition: attention-based AI systems are most effective when embedded within governance structures that preserve human agency, ethical transparency, and collective sensemaking.

Overall, the review positions AI attention mechanisms as transformative catalysts for organisational learning. They shift the dominant paradigm of knowledge management from the accumulation of information towards context-aware, selective, and feedback-driven learning. In doing so, they bridge computational intelligence and human cognition, offering organisations the capacity to learn not only faster but also more intelligently, by focusing attention where it matters most.

5 Theoretical and Practical Implications of AI Attention Mechanisms in Organisational Learning

This section interprets the synthesised findings in light of established theoretical perspectives and situates the review's contribution within ongoing debates in the Information Systems (IS) and organisational learning literature. It discusses (1) how AI attention mechanisms advance theoretical understanding of organisational learning, (2) their implications for practice and management, and (3) the remaining research gaps and directions for future inquiry.

5.1 Theoretical Implications

The findings extend existing theories of organisational learning and knowledge management by introducing attention mechanisms as a bridging construct between cognitive and technological dimensions of learning. Building on the knowledge-based and attention-based views of the firm (Ocasio, 1997; Ocasio et al., 2020), this review shows that AI systems no longer serve merely as information-processing tools but as *agents of attentional allocation* that influence what knowledge is noticed, retained, and acted upon.

In this respect, the review contributes to a more integrated understanding of hybrid attention, where human and algorithmic focus interact dynamically to shape learning outcomes. The concept aligns with practice-theoretical views of situated attention (Nicolini & Mengis, 2024), which emphasise that attentional processes are embedded in socio-material practices rather than confined to individual cognition. By framing AI attention as both a technical and organisational phenomenon, the analysis helps bridge micro-level cognitive theories with macro-level perspectives on knowledge governance.

Furthermore, the review clarifies that attention mechanisms reconfigure organisations' feedback architecture. Rather than operating in linear knowledge cycles, firms adopting attention-based AI increasingly engage in reflexive learning loops, in which human insights recalibrate AI models and algorithmic outputs reshape human sensemaking. This recursive configuration expands the traditional boundaries of organisational learning, offering a richer theoretical account of how feedback and attention jointly sustain adaptive capabilities.

5.2 Managerial and Practical Implications

From a managerial standpoint, the review underscores that AI attention mechanisms can substantially improve knowledge efficiency and strategic responsiveness, provided they are embedded within well-designed governance frameworks. Managers can leverage these systems to prioritise knowledge flows, reduce informational noise, and enhance decision quality. However, realising these benefits requires conscious orchestration of three conditions.

First, human oversight remains indispensable. While attention-based systems can identify relevance with remarkable precision, they cannot assess contextual meaning or ethical implications. Management must therefore institutionalise human checkpoints to validate AI outputs and prevent cognitive or ethical blind spots.

Second, organisations should cultivate feedback literacy, which is the capability of employees to interpret, question, and iteratively refine AI-generated insights. When users treat AI feedback as conversational rather than prescriptive, learning becomes collaborative and self-correcting.

Third, firms should invest in attentional governance by designing mechanisms that align algorithmic focus with strategic priorities. This involves defining what constitutes "relevant knowledge", ensuring that automated attention does not marginalise minority viewpoints or peripheral innovations that could hold future value.

Managerial effectiveness in deploying AI attention systems depends less on technological sophistication and more on the organisational capacity to balance automation with reflection.

5.3 Research Agenda and Future Directions

Although the reviewed studies offer valuable insights, the field remains in its formative stage. Future research should pursue three interrelated directions.

Theory Building and Integration Further conceptual work is needed to unify attention-based mechanisms with existing theories of organisational learning, such as absorptive capacity, knowledge ambidexterity, and digital servitisation. Longitudinal studies could clarify how hybrid attention evolves as AI systems and human routines co-adapt over time.

Empirical Validation and Measurement The predominance of qualitative studies indicates the need for systematic, multi-method research. Quantitative and mixed-methods designs could operationalise constructs such as AI-augmented attention, feedback elasticity, or organisational *attentional balance* to test causal relationships between attention mechanisms and performance outcomes.

Ethical and Socio-Cognitive Boundaries Future investigations should address the normative dimensions of algorithmic attention, namely how power asymmetries, data biases, and transparency issues affect trust and learning quality. Comparative studies across industries and cultures may illuminate how organisational values mediate the acceptance and impact of attention-based AI.

Pursuing these directions would advance a cumulative research programme that links the technical design of attention mechanisms with their human and institutional consequences, enriching both IS theory and organisational practice.

6 Conclusion

This review synthesised 15 peer-reviewed studies to examine how AI attention mechanisms enhance organisational learning, particularly through feedback processes that enable knowledge acquisition and sharing. The analysis revealed that attention mechanisms, developed initially as computational tools in machine learning, have evolved into organisational capabilities that structure how knowledge is prioritised and applied. By filtering and contextualising information, they help organisations manage informational abundance and improve learning efficiency, while also introducing new challenges related to bias, over-reliance, and the erosion of human critical reflection.

In addressing the research question, the review shows that AI attention mechanisms can strengthen organisational learning by transforming feedback from a linear exchange into a reflexive, iterative process between humans and AI systems. This hybrid interaction enables more adaptive and context-aware learning outcomes, in which human cognition and algorithmic attention co-produce insight and knowledge alignment.

Conceptually, the literature review advances the integration of the attention-based and knowledge-based views of the firm, positioning attention as the mechanism that links data processing with organisational sensemaking. Methodologically, it contributes a structured synthesis that connects technical design features of attention with their organisational effects. Together, these contributions offer a foundation for future research on hybrid human–AI attention systems and their implications for sustainable, learning-oriented organisations.

References

Alavi, M., & Leidner, D. (1999). Knowledge management systems: Issues, challenges, and benefits. *Communications of the Association for Information Systems, 1*, 1–37. https://doi.org/10.17705/1CAIS.00107

Alavi, M., Leidner, D. E., & Mousavi, R. (2024). Knowledge management perspective of generative artificial intelligence. *Journal of the Association for Information Systems, 25*(1), 1–12. https://doi.org/10.17705/1JAIS.00859

Bencsik, A. (2021). The sixth generation of knowledge management—The headway of artificial intelligence. *Journal of International Studies, 14*(2), 84–101. https://doi.org/10.14254/2071-8330.2021/14-2/6

Bergmann, D., & Stryker, C. (2024, December 4). What is an attention mechanism? *IBM Think*. Retrieved from https://www.ibm.com/think/topics/attention-mechanism Wikipedia

Budhwar, P., Malik, A., De Silva, M. T. T., & Thevisuthan, P. (2022). Artificial intelligence–challenges and opportunities for international HRM: A review and research agenda. *The International Journal of Human Resource Management, 33*(6), 1065–1097. https://doi.org/10.1080/09585192.2022.2035161

Haefner, N., Wincent, J., Parida, V., & Gassmann, O. (2021). Artificial intelligence and innovation management: A review, framework, and research agenda. *Technological Forecasting and Social Change, 162*, 120392. https://doi.org/10.1016/j.techfore.2020.120392

Jarrahi, M. H., Askay, D., Eshraghi, A., & Smith, P. (2023a). Artificial intelligence and knowledge management: A partnership between human and AI. *Business Horizons, 66*(1), 87–99. https://doi.org/10.1016/j.bushor.2022.03.002

Jarrahi, M. H., Kenyon, S., Brown, A., Donahue, C., & Wicher, C. (2023b). Artificial intelligence: A strategy to harness its power through organizational learning. *Journal of Business Strategy, 44*(3), 126–135. https://doi.org/10.1108/JBS-11-2021-0182

Jo, H., & Park, D.-H. (2024). Effects of ChatGPT's AI capabilities and human-like traits on spreading information in work environments. *Scientific Reports, 14*(1), Article 7806. https://doi.org/10.1038/s41598-024-57977-0

Johns, G. (2006). The essential impact of context on organizational behavior. *Academy of Management Review, 31*(2), 386–408. https://doi.org/10.5465/amr.2006.20208687

Kaczorowska-Spychalska, D., Kotula, N., Mazurek, G., & Sułkowski, Ł. (2024). Generative AI as source of change of knowledge management paradigm. *Human Technology, 20*(1), 131–154. https://doi.org/10.14254/1795-6889.2024.20-1.7

Kostis, A., Lidstrom, J., Nair, S., & Holmstrom, J. (2024). Too much AI hype, too little emphasis on learning? Entrepreneurs designing business models through learning-by-conversing with generative AI. *IEEE Transactions on Engineering Management*. Advance online publication. https://doi.org/10.1109/TEM.2024.3484750

Leoni, L., Gueli, G., Ardolino, M., Panizzon, M., & Gupta, S. (2024). AI-empowered KM processes for decision-making: Empirical evidence from worldwide organisations. *Journal of Knowledge Management, 28*(11), 320–347. https://doi.org/10.1108/JKM-03-2024-0262

Mancuso, I., Petruzzelli, A. M., Panniello, U., & Frattini, F. (2025). The role of explainable artificial intelligence (XAI) in innovation processes: A knowledge management perspective. *Technology in Society, 82*, 102909. https://doi.org/10.1016/j.techsoc.2025.102909

Myers, M. D., & Klein, H. K. (2011). A set of principles for conducting critical research in information systems. *MIS Quarterly, 35*(1), 17–36. https://doi.org/10.2307/23043487

Nicolini, D., & Mengis, J. (2024). Toward a practice-theoretical view of the situated nature of attention. *Strategic Organization, 22*(1), 211–234. https://doi.org/10.1177/14761270231183731

Nonaka, I. (1994). A dynamic theory of organizational knowledge creation. *Organization Science, 5*(1), 14–37. https://doi.org/10.1287/orsc.5.1.14

Ocasio, W. (1997). Towards an Attention Based View of the Firm. *Strategic Management Journal, 18*, 187–206. https://doi.org/10.1002/(SICI)1097-0266(199707)18:1+187::AID-SMJ9363.3.CO;2-B

Ocasio, W., Rhee, L., & Milner, D. (2020). Attention, knowledge, and organizational learning. In L. Argote & J. M. Levine (Eds.), *The Oxford handbook of group and organizational learning* (pp. 81–94). Oxford University Press. https://doi.org/10.1093/oxfordhb/9780190263362.013.33

Olan, F., Ogiemwonyi Arakpogun, E., Suklan, J., Nakpodia, F., Damij, N., & Jayawickrama, U. (2022). Artificial intelligence and knowledge sharing: Contributing factors to organizational performance. *Journal of Business Research, 145*, 605–615. https://doi.org/10.1016/j.jbusres.2022.03.008

Ramaul, L., Ritala, P., & Ruokonen, M. (2024). Creational and conversational AI affordances: How the new breed of chatbots is revolutionizing knowledge industries. *Business Horizons, 67*(5), 615–627. https://doi.org/10.1016/j.bushor.2024.05.006

Retkowsky, J., Hafermalz, E., & Huysman, M. (2024). Managing a ChatGPT-empowered workforce: Understanding its affordances and side effects. *Business Horizons, 67*(5), 511–523. https://doi.org/10.1016/j.bushor.2024.04.009

Ritala, P., Aaltonen, P., Ruokonen, M., & Nemeh, A. (2024). Developing industrial AI capabilities: An organisational learning perspective. *Technovation, 138*, 103120. https://doi.org/10.1016/j.technovation.2024.103120

Sumbal, M. S., Amber, Q., Tariq, A., Raziq, M. M., & Tsui, E. (2024). Wind of change: How ChatGPT and big data can reshape the knowledge management paradigm? *Industrial Management & Data Systems, 124*(9), 2736–2757. https://doi.org/10.1108/IMDS-06-2023-0360

Tetrick, L. E., & Camburn, M. K. (2004). Organizational structure. In C. D. Spielberger (Ed.), *Encyclopedia of applied psychology* (Vol. 2, pp. 747–753). Elsevier Academic Press. https://doi.org/10.1016/B0-12-657410-3/00525-0

Tsoi, J. C.-H., & Strønen, F. H. (2024). Integration of conversational AI capabilities in knowledge management processes for higher education. In *Proceedings of the 25th European Conference on Knowledge Management* (pp. 1026–1033). Academic Conferences International. https://doi.org/10.34190/eckm.25.1.2659

vom Brocke, J., Simons, A., Riemer, K., Niehaves, B., Plattfaut, R., & Cleven, A. (2015). Standing on the shoulders of giants: Challenges and recommendations of literature search in information systems research. *Communications of the Association for Information Systems, 37*, Article 9, 205–224. https://doi.org/10.17705/1CAIS.03709

Wijnhoven, F. (2022). Organizational learning for intelligence amplification adoption: Lessons from a clinical decision support system adoption project. *Information Systems Frontiers, 24*(3), 731–744. https://doi.org/10.1007/s10796-021-10206-9

Hybrid Attention in Decision-Making

AI-Augmented Attention in Organizational Decision-Making

Emma Bongartz, Marlene Heinemann, and Isabel Ramos

Declarations

- ChatGPT was used to improve the final quality of the text. ChatGPT was also used to identify the initial search strings for the articles to be included in the first phase of the literature review. The authors later refined these initial strings through successive adjustments and verification of the results. The authors reviewed and take full responsibility for the content of this chapter.

1 Introduction

Organizations today operate in increasingly complex and data-intensive environments where decision-making requires both analytical rigor and contextual sensitivity. Artificial intelligence (AI), and particularly generative artificial intelligence (GenAI), has emerged as a powerful enabler in this regard, offering unprecedented capacity to process large-scale data, identify patterns, and prioritize relevant signals. At the same time, organizational decision-making cannot rely solely on computational capabilities: it also depends on human insight, encompassing intuition, contextual reasoning, and ethical judgment. This duality highlights the importance of exploring how AI attention mechanisms, designed to filter and focus on salient information, can complement, rather than replace, human attentional and cognitive processes in organizational contexts.

E. Bongartz · M. Heinemann
Department of Information Systems, University of Münster, Münster, Germany
e-mail: ebongart@uni-muenster.de; mheinema@uni-muenster.de

I. Ramos (✉)
Department of Information Systems, University of Minho, Guimarães, Portugal
e-mail: iramos@dsi.uminho.pt

I. Ramos et al. (eds.), *Hybrid Attention in Organizations*, SpringerBriefs in Information Systems, https://doi.org/10.1007/978-3-032-30186-4_2

The growing body of scholarship on human–AI collaboration suggests that the interplay between machine precision and human judgment holds significant promise for improving decision quality, timeliness, and accountability (Dellermann et al., 2019; Ngoc & Elbanna, 2023; Steyvers & Kumar, 2024; Ramos & Barros, 2024). However, this promise is accompanied by challenges, including risks of overreliance on AI, erosion of human agency, and unresolved concerns about trust, transparency, and bias. These tensions underscore the need for a systematic examination of the conditions under which AI-augmented attention contributes positively to organizational outcomes.

This chapter addresses this need by conducting a systematic literature review (SLR) of peer-reviewed studies published between 2020 and 2025. The guiding research question is: *How can AI attention mechanisms complement human insights in organizations?* Four specific objectives structure this inquiry: (1) to clarify and define the concepts of AI-augmented attention and human insights in organizational decision-making; (2) to identify empirical findings and evidence on their interaction; (3) to reveal current gaps and contradictions in the literature; and (4) to provide a grounded synthesis of findings and avenues for future research. Together, these objectives seek to advance theoretical understanding and provide actionable implications for practice.

By systematically mapping existing research, this study contributes to the field of information systems in three ways. First, it consolidates conceptual and empirical insights into the complementarity between AI and human attentional processes, addressing a fragmented, rapidly evolving literature. Second, it highlights the managerial and organizational conditions that enable responsible and effective use of AI in decision-making, thereby informing practice. Third, it outlines an agenda for future research, emphasizing the need for stronger theoretical foundations, broader empirical validation, and actionable recommendations for management. In doing so, the chapter positions AI-augmented attention as a socio-technical phenomenon, where organizational outcomes depend not only on technological design but also on human interpretation, trust, and accountability.

2 Planning and Implementing the Systematic Literature Review

This study follows a structured PRISMA-inspired process (Page et al., 2021) to ensure transparency, reproducibility, and rigor in all stages of the SLR. Each phase—identification, screening, eligibility, and inclusion—is reported with quantitative details and procedural explanations.

2.1 Search Strategy and Identification Procedures

The review began with the definition of research questions and the establishment of boundaries for the search. The guiding research question of this review is: *How can AI attention mechanisms complement human insights in organizations?* This question is supported by four objectives: (1) clarifying and defining the concepts of AI-augmented attention and human insights in organizational decision-making; (2) identifying empirical evidence on their relationship and interaction; (3) revealing current gaps and contradictions in the literature; and (4) offering a grounded synthesis of findings and avenues for future research. Together, these elements are highly relevant for both theoretical and practical reasons. Conceptual clarification is essential, as existing studies often employ fragmented definitions that hinder cumulative knowledge building. Identifying empirical evidence enables the field to move beyond abstract discussions toward an assessment of AI's actual impact on decision-making. Highlighting gaps and contradictions addresses the current fragmentation in theoretical perspectives and methodological approaches, providing direction for more robust, generalizable insights. Finally, synthesizing results and mapping future research opportunities not only advances the scholarly understanding of AI–human collaboration but also equips managers with evidence-based guidance for integrating AI responsibly. By uniting these objectives, the research question ensures that the review contributes to a nuanced understanding of how AI attention mechanisms in GenAI tools can act as a complement rather than a substitute for human judgment, thereby shaping decision-making processes that are both more efficient and more accountable.

To operationalize the research question, an initial search string was developed based on the SPIDER framework (Cooke et al., 2012), ensuring alignment between the key concepts of AI attention mechanisms, human insights, and organizational decision-making. This narrow query was designed to maximize precision and retrieve publications that directly addressed the interplay between human and AI contributions to decision-making. The following example illustrates the core search string applied in the first stage of the review.

(TITLE-ABS-KEY ("decision-maker" OR "manager" OR "organizations") AND TITLE-ABS-KEY ("AI Attention mechanisms" OR "human insight in organizations") AND TITLE-ABS-KEY ("impact" OR "benefit" OR "support"))

Following the initial search, test runs revealed that the initial queries were either too narrow, yielding very few results, or too broad, producing unmanageable outputs. To address this problem, refinements were introduced in line with best practices for systematic reviews, gradually broadening the Phenomenon of Interest while keeping strict conceptual alignment with the research objectives. Through this iterative process, two refined search strings (Levels B-3 and B-5) were identified as optimal, striking a balance between breadth and precision. These strings were subsequently applied across all databases to ensure robust and comparable coverage.

- *Level B-3 (Refined)*:
  (TITLE-ABS-KEY ("decision-maker" OR "manager" OR "organizations") AND TITLE-ABS-KEY ("AI" OR "artificial intelligence" OR "machine learning") AND TITLE-ABS-KEY ("decision-making" OR "judgment" OR "human insight"))
- *Level B-5 (Refined)*:
  (TITLE-ABS-KEY ("organization*" OR "manager*") AND TITLE-ABS-KEY ("AI" OR "artificial intelligence" OR "machine learning") AND TITLE-ABS-KEY ("decision-making" OR "judgment" OR "insight" OR "support"))

These refinements expanded the coverage to capture studies using broader terminology while maintaining relevance to the core focus of AI attention mechanisms and human insights in organizational decision-making.

After defining and refining the search strings, the next step involved applying them across the selected academic databases to systematically retrieve relevant literature. To ensure comprehensive coverage of scholarship in information systems, management, and computer science, three major databases were selected based on their recognized breadth and disciplinary relevance: Scopus, AIS eLibrary, and IEEE Xplore. The searches yielded the following initial results:

- *Scopus*: 86 records retrieved
- *AIS eLibrary*: 69 records retrieved
- *IEEE Xplore*: 143 records retrieved

This initial stage yielded *298 records*. To mitigate the risk of omitting influential contributions not indexed in these databases, we applied backward and forward snowballing of key references, which led to the identification of four additional studies. Consequently, a total of *302 records* were included in the initial processing.

2.2 Screening of Retrieved Records

The retrieved records were imported into Zotero for reference management and automatic duplicate detection. After duplicate removal, *239 unique records* remained. Screening was conducted using Rayyan, a specialized tool for collaborative systematic reviews, which allowed blind and independent screening by two reviewers to reduce bias.

At this stage, inclusion and exclusion criteria were operationalized. Records were retained if they (a) addressed artificial intelligence in organizational or socio-technical contexts, (b) were published in peer-reviewed venues, and (c) provided conceptual, empirical, or methodological contributions. Exclusion criteria encompassed purely technical studies with no organizational relevance, non-peer-reviewed sources, and papers outside the scope of attention, cognition, or organizational processes.

- Records screened by title and abstract: 239
- Records excluded: 183 (for reasons such as lack of organizational focus, insufficient conceptual contribution, or publication in non-scholarly outlets)

  This process resulted in *56 records* advancing to the eligibility phase.

2.3 Eligibility Assessment of Full-Text Articles

In the eligibility stage, *56 full-text articles* were retrieved and carefully examined. Each article was assessed against quality criteria to ensure that only methodologically rigorous and conceptually clear studies were retained. These criteria included:

1. *Conceptual clarity*: explicit definitions of constructs and theoretical positioning.
2. *Methodological rigor*: transparent research design, appropriate use of data and analysis methods.
3. *Scholarly reputation*: publication in journals or conferences recognized in the fields of information systems, management, or human–computer interaction.

The evaluation was conducted independently by two reviewers, and divergences were resolved by consensus. Importantly, no article was excluded at this stage as all 56 studies met the minimum eligibility standards, though the level of methodological sophistication varied across the corpus.

2.4 Study Inclusion and Final Sample

Ultimately, *56 studies* were included in the final systematic literature review. Given the exploratory and conceptual nature of the research objectives, a meta-analysis was not conducted. Instead, we employed a mixed descriptive and thematic synthesis. The descriptive synthesis summarized publication patterns (e.g., outlets, years, methods), while the thematic synthesis identified core conceptual categories, emerging trends, and theoretical gaps. This dual approach allowed us to provide both an overview of the field and deeper insights into the conceptual landscape (Table 1).

2.5 Reflections on the Implemented SLR Process

Although the systematic process was designed to maximize rigor, certain limitations must be acknowledged. First, the reliance on three databases (Scopus, AIS eLibrary, and IEEE Xplore) may have led to the exclusion of relevant studies indexed elsewhere. Second, the review focused exclusively on publications written in English, which may limit the cultural and geographical diversity of the included

Table 1 Overview of records across the PRISMA-inspired review phase

Phase	Records considered	Excluded (with reasons)	Notes
Identification	302 (298 from databases + 4 from other sources)	–	Scopus = 86; AIS = 69; IEEE = 143
Screening	239	183 (duplicated, not relevant, non-peer-reviewed, or purely technical)	Screened by title/abstract in Rayyan
Eligibility	56	0	All met quality criteria
Inclusion	56 full-text	–	Included in final SLR; no meta-analysis performed

perspectives. Third, while backward and forward snowballing mitigated database limitations, they cannot guarantee full coverage of gray literature or emerging work in preprints. Finally, although independent screening and consensus discussions enhanced reliability, subjective judgments in applying inclusion/exclusion and quality criteria remain inherent to any review process. Recognizing these constraints reinforces the transparency of our approach and allows readers to interpret the findings with an informed understanding of the review's scope and boundaries.

3 Synthesis and Reporting of Review Findings

The final stage of the review involved the systematic reporting and documentation of results. This stage was essential to ensure both transparency and replicability, two central principles of high-quality literature reviews (Okoli, 2015; Page et al., 2021).

3.1 Synthesis Strategy

To integrate the evidence retrieved, a structured synthesis approach was adopted, combining descriptive and conceptual analysis. In line with established methodological recommendations (Vom Brocke et al., 2015; Webster & Watson, 2002), the synthesis proceeded in three steps. First, a thematic synthesis was conducted, grouping studies by common concepts, methods, and findings to highlight convergences and discrepancies. Second, concept mapping was employed to visualize the interrelationships between findings, particularly in terms of whether results supported, contradicted, or extended each other (Klein et al., 2007). Finally, a descriptive analysis provided quantitative insights into the distribution of studies, for example, by year of publication, methodological design, or theoretical foundation. This combination of approaches allowed for a comprehensive and nuanced synthesis of the state of knowledge.

3.2 *Documenting the Review Process*

The reporting phase also entailed a systematic documentation of each procedural step, ensuring replicability and auditability. All screening decisions were recorded, quality assessments were transparently reported, and data extraction was standardized through structured templates. This documentation captured the evolution of search strategies, refinements made to query strings, and the criteria applied during pre-selection and eligibility screening. Regular updates of the documentation process provided a clear overview of progress and ensured that methodological rigor was consistently maintained throughout.

3.3 *Summary of Findings*

In total, *56 studies* met the inclusion and quality requirements and were subjected to detailed synthesis. As illustrated in Fig. 1, the studies were classified into five core thematic clusters: (1) AI–human collaboration in decision-making; (2) trust and acceptance factors; (3) organizational integration and effects of AI; (4) AI support for human performance and evaluation; and (5) ethical and legal issues. An additional group of studies was classified as "other" due to their peripheral relevance. This categorization provides a structured overview of the current state of research and highlights the thematic diversity of the field.

Methodologically, the body of literature reflects the exploratory nature of GenAI-supported decision-making in organizations. Of the included studies, 20% employed quantitative methods, 38% qualitative methods, and 43% mixed-methods designs. This distribution suggests a strong reliance on interpretive and exploratory approaches, aimed at uncovering mechanisms, perceptions, and contextual factors rather than producing generalizable causal claims. The theoretical landscape was equally fragmented, as 57% of studies did not explicitly apply a theoretical

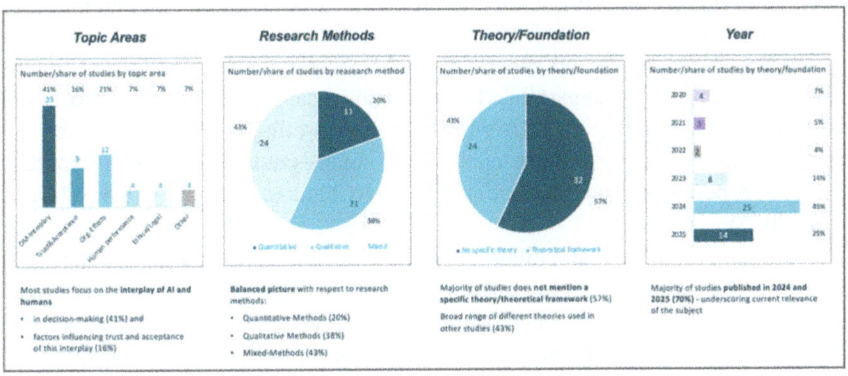

Fig. 1 Thematic classification of the 56 studies included in the review

framework, while the remaining contributions drew on a heterogeneous set of theories spanning management, psychology, cognitive science, and information systems (e.g., Resource-Based View Theory, Self-Determination Theory, Organizational Information Processing Theory). Such variety underscores both the richness of the domain and the absence of a unifying theoretical lens.

Finally, the temporal distribution of publications demonstrates the field's novelty and rapid growth. More than 70% of included studies were published in 2024 or 2025, reflecting the recent surge of scholarly interest in AI-augmented decision-making and confirming the timeliness of this review.

4 Discussion: Key Insights from the Current State of Research

This section synthesizes the findings of the reviewed studies by grouping them into five thematic areas. Each subsection concludes with a reflection on how the identified insights inform the guiding research question: "*How can AI attention mechanisms complement human insights in organizations?*"

4.1 Content-Related Findings in Core Thematic Areas

As highlighted before, five core thematic areas have been identified. The key findings related to each area are summarized in the sections below.

AI–Human Collaboration: Decision-Making-Interplay

A considerable number of studies explore how the combination of artificial intelligence (AI) and human insight can lead to more effective decisions and decision-making (Boyacı et al., 2024; Chanda, 2024; Molina et al., 2024).

The key drivers behind this synergy lie in the complementary strengths of humans and AI. While AI offers unparalleled computational capabilities (such as processing large datasets, generating data-driven insights, performing predictive analytics, and running simulations or scenario analyses), humans contribute domain expertise, practical experience, and intuitive judgment (Chaturvedi et al., 2025; Masaeid et al., 2025).

The nature of AI–human collaboration in decision-making varies depending on the type of decision context. In structured, repetitive decision-making environments where clear rules and historical data are available, AI can deliver efficient, accurate decisions. In these cases, humans primarily assume a supervisory role, ensuring that AI systems function within ethical, legal, and organizational boundaries. In contrast, unstructured and non-repetitive decision contexts, marked by uncertainty, novelty, or the absence of relevant data, require a human-centered approach. In such situations, AI serves as a supportive assistant, offering computational power and analytical input, while humans retain full control over judgment and final decision-making (Aal, 2025; Steyvers & Kumar, 2024; Trunk et al., 2020).

In this context, Aal (2025) presents a typology of four decision-making scenarios and respective decision-quality oversight actions, structured along two dimensions: the level of complexity (low/transparent vs. high/non-transparent) and the locus of decision-making (AI vs. human). In cases where AI systems operate autonomously and complexity is low, decision quality is ensured through regular technical checks ("*Technical Oversight*"). When AI acts autonomously in high-complexity environments, oversight involves a broader range of human experts from various business units to maintain decision quality ("*Business Oversight*"). In contrast, when complexity is low and humans make the final decision based on AI recommendations, decision quality is supported by a critical human mindset and a basic understanding of how the AI system generates its suggestions ("*Informed Reliance*"). In high-complexity scenarios where humans retain decision-making authority with AI support, decision quality is safeguarded through "*Supervised Reliance*," which includes systematic and comprehensive review processes. Complementary work similarly emphasises that AI-augmented decision-making must be designed as a human–organisational activity, with explicit decision rights, validation routines, and managerial responsibility for final decisions (Herath Pathirannehelage et al., 2025; Meyer, 2024; Tabesh, 2022).

Other studies offer examples and case studies that explore the interaction between AI and humans in decision-making. Steyvers and Kumar (2024), for instance, highlight both the potentials and challenges through real-world applications. For example, they note that in clinical decision support systems, AI attention mechanisms can identify cases that doctors might miss. At the same time, human expertise plays a crucial role in assessing the quality and reliability of AI-generated alerts, particularly in relation to different diseases or specific patient subpopulations.

Several studies emphasize that when AI mechanisms complement human insights in decision-making, both the quality of decisions and the effectiveness of decision-making processes can be enhanced (Choi et al., 2025; Goel & Mahur, 2025; Neiroukh et al., 2024; Ines et al., 2024). Regarding decision quality and accuracy, Choi et al. (2025) draw on empirical data from the strategic board game "*Go*" and demonstrate a significant improvement in move quality among players who use and learn from an AI support system. This effect is particularly strong in the early stages of the game, characterized by high uncertainty, which allows one to outperform even professional players.

Goel and Mahur (2025) examine the influence of GenAI on business analytics and decision-making within service organizations. Their findings suggest that integrating GenAI techniques with traditional business analytics frameworks leads to substantial gains in decision effectiveness (i.e., predictive accuracy) and, at the same time, improves the efficiency of decision-making processes (i.e., operational performance).

Similarly, Neiroukh et al. (2024), as well as Ines et al. (2024), based on a survey of 184 companies and 100 SMEs, respectively, provide evidence that the use of AI capabilities not only enhances business performance through better decision quality but also improves the overall effectiveness of decision-making processes by enabling more timely decisions.

Evidence indicates that AI systems excel at structured, repetitive tasks, where computational speed and accuracy are critical, while humans excel at contextual reasoning, intuition, and ethical judgment in more ambiguous or unstructured contexts. Studies demonstrate that this complementarity not only enhances decision quality but also reduces biases and improves timeliness. Thus, the literature shows that the interplay between human expertise and AI capabilities creates hybrid decision systems that outperform either actor alone. These findings directly inform the research question by demonstrating that AI mechanisms complement human insights most effectively when tasks are distributed according to each party's comparative strengths.

AI–Human Collaboration: Trust and Acceptance Factors

According to the theory of algorithmic aversion, people generally place greater trust in human-made decisions than in those generated by AI (Glienke et al., 2023; Keding & Meissner, 2021). Against this backdrop, several studies have examined factors that positively or negatively influence trust and acceptance of decisions arising from various forms of AI–human collaboration.

Assuming that trust is a key driver for the adoption of AI and for realizing its full potential, Baduna and Hylving (2023) investigate how trust develops in AI-augmented decision-making systems within collaborative environments. Based on a comprehensive literature review, they identify four key antecedents of human trust in collaboration with AI: (1) Human Characteristics (e.g., experience, expertise, self-confidence); (2) AI Characteristics (e.g., quality of training data, transparency, explainability); (3) Decision-Making Environment (e.g., organizational incentives, role clarity); (4) Collaboration Setting (e.g., task configuration, degree of autonomy). This framework is supported by further studies focusing on these antecedents individually.

Regarding human characteristics, Haesevoets et al. (2021) identify four distinct types of managers, each with different preferences for AI–human collaboration. Group 1 (5%) prefers a partnership in which machines have the upper hand in managerial decisions, whereas Group 2 (15%) prefers a setting with equal input of humans and machines. Group 3 (50%) prefers humans to have a majority vote in management decisions; Group 4 (30%) wants humans to retain full control. The study suggests that individual decision-making styles and cognitive patterns of executives shape the degree of trust and acceptance toward AI-supported decisions.

Keding and Meissner (2021) show that executives' attitudes toward predominantly AI-driven advice vary depending on the decision-making environment. Their findings from a vignette-based decision experiment with 150 senior executives on R&D investments suggest that AI-generated recommendations are perceived as more reliable than those from human advisors for objective, analytical tasks. In these situations, the phenomenon of algorithmic aversion may reverse into algorithmic appreciation, creating a risk of overreliance on AI-based recommendations.

Beyond human characteristics and the decision-making environment, trust in AI recommendations complementing human insight is strongly influenced by AI characteristics and the collaboration setting. Key factors influencing trust and adoption of AI-augmented decision-making include transparency about the amount and quality of data used, the interpretability of AI recommendations (e.g., clarity, visualizations), the explainability and comprehensibility of underlying algorithms as well as the level of autonomy given to AI in decision-making (Glienke et al., 2023; Janhunen et al., 2024; Schemmer et al., 2022; Zhang et al., 2024).

Research highlights key antecedents of trust, including human characteristics (e.g., expertise, decision-making style), AI characteristics (e.g., explainability, transparency), and organizational context (e.g., incentives, role clarity). Studies further reveal that trust dynamics influence the balance between algorithmic aversion and algorithmic appreciation. Without sufficient trust, AI recommendations are underutilized; conversely, excessive trust risks overreliance. Therefore, insights into trust and acceptance illuminate the social and psychological conditions under which AI attention mechanisms can responsibly complement human insights in organizations, ensuring that collaboration yields balanced and accountable decisions.

GenAI: Organizational Integration and Effects

The content and findings of the studies included in this SLR clearly demonstrate that various forms of AI–human interaction in decision-making have already become established practice across many organizations. A broad range of case studies, empirical investigations, and expert interviews evidence this.

The integration of AI to complement human insight with respect to organizational decision-making reveals two key dimensions of impact. On the one hand, it serves as a catalyst for organizational transformation. The use of AI in conjunction with human insight reshapes employee behavior, alters interpersonal dynamics, and contributes to a shift in organizational culture, fostering new ways of thinking, working, and interacting (Kheterpal et al., 2024; Lim & Ravesangar, 2025).

Drawing on both qualitative and quantitative data from leaders, managers, and employees, Sharma and Reddy (2024) demonstrate that the successful integration of AI into organizations is more likely when the purpose and objectives of AI implementation are clearly communicated across all levels of the organization. Furthermore, upskilling and reskilling initiatives are essential to prepare employees for their evolving roles and responsibilities in working with AI. Employee acceptance and engagement tend to increase when concerns about job security are acknowledged and addressed as part of the organizational change process.

On the other hand, the collaboration between AI and humans is increasingly recognized as a strategic driver of value across organizations. In terms of economic impact, one of the most prominent benefits lies in the substantial improvements in operational efficiency. Evidence from various industries (including manufacturing, healthcare, and customer service) shows that AI can streamline operations. These include, for example, reduced downtimes through predictive maintenance, automated quality control through expert systems (Scarton et al., 2025), optimized production planning, and more efficient handling of customer inquiries via intelligent automation. Beyond operational gains, AI-supported decision-making and process optimization can also contribute to revenue growth. This occurs through improved allocation of marketing budgets, more precise targeting, and increased conversion rates. At a strategic level, integrating AI into decision-making processes unlocks new avenues for competitive advantage. AI can enable the development of innovative products and services, support the identification of emerging trends, and facilitate creative problem-solving. In this way, AI becomes a catalyst for long-term value creation and strategic differentiation (Ines et al., 2024; Akhunova et al., 2024).

Beyond individual decision processes, AI integration reshapes organizational structures and cultures. Studies show that effective adoption depends on transparent communication of AI's role, reskilling initiatives, and alignment with strategic goals. Benefits include improved operational efficiency, predictive maintenance, enhanced targeting, and innovative product development. However, integration also requires organizational change management to address employee concerns and ensure responsible use. These findings contribute to demonstrating that AI complements human insights not only at the micro level of decision-making but also by transforming organizational processes and creating conditions that enable human–AI synergies to flourish.

GenAI: Support of Human Performance

In addition to organizational dynamics, a growing body of research emphasizes the individual-level implications of AI–human collaboration in decision-making. These studies examine how AI augments human cognitive capabilities, enhances individual performance, and transforms how people engage with complex decision-making tasks. By complementing human strengths, AI systems not only support more effective outcomes but also influence how individuals interact with information, assume responsibility, and adapt their decision strategies in AI-enhanced environments.

AI–human collaboration holds significant potential to enhance individual effectiveness by improving the speed, accuracy, and consistency of decisions. It enables employees to make better-informed choices, reduces cognitive load, and helps mitigate common human errors such as biases, oversights, or fatigue-related mistakes (Carter & Liu, 2025).

At the same time, the integration of AI into decision-making processes is transforming traditional job profiles. As routine tasks become increasingly automated, the skill sets required of employees are shifting. Analytical thinking, data literacy, and the ability to interpret and critically assess AI-generated outputs are becoming essential competencies (Manoharan et al., 2024).

As routine tasks are increasingly automated, human roles shift toward tasks requiring interpretation, contextualization, and strategic oversight. This stream illustrates how AI mechanisms act as complementary tools that amplify, rather than replace, human cognitive strengths, thereby enabling employees to focus on higher-order insights and judgment.

GenAI: Ethical and Legal Issues

A final group of studies explores the ethical and legal implications of using AI to complement human judgment in decision-making processes. These contributions highlight not only critical concerns but also the resulting challenges that organizations must actively confront in order to ensure responsible and trustworthy AI use (Alsumayt et al., 2024; Reddy et al., 2024).

Among the most frequently cited concerns are the risk of data privacy violations and the potential misuse of sensitive information. As AI systems rely heavily on large volumes of personal and organizational data, ensuring robust data governance and compliance with legal standards becomes essential.

Another key issue is the erosion of human agency and accountability. As decision-making responsibilities shift toward algorithmic systems, there is a growing risk of diminishing human oversight and personal responsibility. This can lead to a lack of clarity around who is ultimately accountable for decisions, especially in high-stakes or ethically sensitive contexts.

Finally, several studies point to algorithms' susceptibility to bias and manipulation. If AI systems are trained on skewed or incomplete data (or intentionally influenced), they may produce non-neutral, biased, or even discriminatory outcomes, undermining the fairness and objectivity of decisions (Mou et al., 2024; Reddy et al., 2024).

Together, these findings underscore the importance of establishing clear ethical guidelines, transparent processes, and legal safeguards to ensure that AI–human collaboration in decision-making aligns with both societal values and organizational accountability standards. Consequently, attention to ethical and legal concerns clarifies the conditions under which AI can meaningfully and responsibly complement human decision-making, ensuring that complementarity strengthens, rather than weakens, organizational accountability and trust.

Taken together, the five thematic areas provide a comprehensive answer to the guiding research question: *How can AI attention mechanisms complement human insights in organizations?* The evidence demonstrates that AI contributes computational efficiency, scalability, and the ability to process vast data environments, while humans provide contextual reasoning, intuition, and ethical oversight. The interplay between these strengths is conditioned by trust and acceptance, organizational integration, individual performance support, and ethical safeguards. When these factors are aligned, AI does not substitute but rather amplifies human insight, enabling organizations to achieve decision-making processes that are more efficient, accurate, and accountable. Thus, the literature suggests that the complementarity of AI attention mechanisms and human judgment constitutes a socio-technical partnership, in which organizational outcomes are optimized through the deliberate orchestration of machine precision and human wisdom.

5 Managerial Implications

Successfully integrating AI into organizational decision-making requires more than simply deploying a new technology or IT system. To ensure that AI mechanisms effectively complement human insight and judgment, a structured change management approach is essential.

As highlighted in the current literature, there is a lack of concrete recommendations and conceptual frameworks to guide this transformation from a management perspective. To address this gap, Kotter's Eight Steps of Change is used as a guiding framework in this article (Kotter, 1995, 2014). It provides a structured pathway for aligning AI adoption with organizational goals and human decision-making processes.

Table 2 outlines each step, accompanied by specific management implications and their rationale based on our research findings.

6 Conclusion

This systematic literature review explored the guiding question: "How *can AI attention mechanisms complement human insights in organizations?*" By analyzing 56 peer-reviewed studies published between 2020 and 2025, the review highlights that

Table 2 Managerial implications for AI–human collaboration mapped onto Kotter's Eight Steps of Change

Step	Management implications	Rationale
Create a sense of urgency	Communicate clearly why AI is being introduced, highlighting its potential to reduce uncertainty, accelerate decisions, and improve outcomes. Link this to concrete competitive pressures and success stories, while explaining how AI will support, rather than replace, employees' work	Creating urgency around AI opportunities and external pressures increases attention, commitment and openness to change, while proactively addressing fears about job loss or role changes reduces resistance and supports early engagement with AI-augmented decision-making (e.g., Sharma & Reddy, 2024)
Build a guiding coalition	Assemble a cross-functional leadership team from IT, HR, operations and business units to sponsor AI–human collaboration. This coalition steers use-case selection, allocates resources, and coordinates technical, organizational, and ethical perspectives on AI-augmented decision-making	A diverse guiding coalition provides the expertise needed for effective oversight of AI outputs, prevents overreliance on purely technical views (e.g., Aal, 2025), and ensures that AI initiatives remain aligned with strategic priorities, organizational capabilities and stakeholder expectations (e.g., Chaturvedi et al., 2025)

(continued)

Table 2 (continued)

Step	Management implications	Rationale
Form a strategic vision and initiatives	Define a clear vision for how AI will complement, not replace, human insight in decision-making. Specify priority use cases, expected benefits, and measurable goals for efficiency, timeliness and quality, and embed these in an implementation roadmap communicated across the organization	A shared strategic vision and concrete initiatives (transparent roadmap) increase transparency, reduce ambiguity about AI's role, and enable systematic tracking of outcomes (by defining KPIs, for example), thereby strengthening acceptance, learning, and continuous improvement of AI-supported decision processes (e.g., Sharma & Reddy, 2024; Ines et al., 2024; Akhunova et al., 2024)
Enlist a volunteer army	Identify and empower early adopters, pilot teams and technology champions at different organizational levels. Involve them in experimenting with AI tools, sharing experiences, and demonstrating how AI can usefully complement human judgment in real decision situations	Volunteer champions create credible, context-specific examples of AI–human collaboration, help diffuse knowledge and enthusiasm, and encourage peers to explore AI support, thereby accelerating adoption beyond formal top-down mandates (e.g., Kotter, 2014)
Enable action by removing barriers	Invest in training and upskilling so employees can interpret AI outputs; adapt incentives to reward informed AI use; and ensure systems provide sufficient transparency, explainability, and appropriate autonomy to support responsible human–AI collaboration	Addressing skill gaps, misaligned incentives and opaque systems reduces distrust and misuse of AI, supports the development of calibrated reliance on AI recommendations, and creates conditions in which human expertise and AI capabilities can be effectively combined (e.g., Glienke et al., 2023; Janhunen et al., 2024; Sharma & Reddy, 2024; Chaturvedi et al., 2025)
Generate short-term wins	Design focused pilot projects where AI can quickly demonstrate measurable improvements in decision quality, speed, or efficiency. Publicize these early successes, along with lessons learned, to reinforce momentum and justify continued investment in AI-augmented decision-making	Visible short-term wins provide tangible evidence that AI–human collaboration creates value, build confidence among skeptical stakeholders, and help secure ongoing support, resources and attention for broader organizational roll-out (e.g., Kotter, 2014)
Sustain acceleration	Scale up successful AI use cases, refine collaboration practices, and regularly review AI performance and human oversight mechanisms. Use user and stakeholder feedback to adjust processes, governance, and training to deepen and broaden AI-supported decision-making	Continuous scaling, review and adjustment prevent stagnation, reduce the risk of overreliance on early designs, and ensure that AI–human collaboration evolves with organizational goals, regulatory changes and emerging ethical expectations (e.g., Kotter, 2014; Aal, 2025)

(continued)

Table 2 (continued)

Step	Management implications	Rationale
Institute change	Formalize AI–human collaboration through policies, guidelines, and role descriptions that define where AI supports decisions, how results are reviewed, what skills are required, and which ethical and legal principles govern AI use across the organization	Embedding AI-related practices into governance structures, compliance processes, and job designs institutionalizes responsible AI use, safeguards accountability, and ensures that AI complements human insight in a consistent, transparent, and legally compliant manner (e.g., Reddy et al., 2024; Alsumayt et al., 2024; Tabesh, 2022)

AI attention mechanisms can significantly improve the quality and efficiency of decision-making in organizations. Crucially, acceptance of AI support hinges on trust, with AI viewed not only as a technological enabler but also as a strategic driver of organizational transformation and value.

The complementary strengths of AI and humans, AI's capacity to handle large-scale structured data and humans' intuitive reasoning, contextual awareness, and ethical judgment, create valuable synergies. Nonetheless, the review highlights key risks, including that overreliance on AI may undermine human agency, reduce accountability, and perpetuate biases, especially in the absence of transparency and explainability. Therefore, effective human–AI collaboration demands careful integration, trust-building measures, and safeguards that preserve human oversight and responsibility.

This study contributes to the information systems domain by mapping current research into five thematic clusters, revealing methodological patterns, and identifying a fragmented theoretical landscape. It also underscores the pressing need for unified conceptual frameworks to advance the understanding of AI-supported decision-making in organizations.

Looking forward, research on AI–human collaboration in organizational decision-making should advance along three interrelated directions. First, future work must prioritize the development of coherent theoretical foundations and conceptual frameworks (Chaturvedi et al., 2025). The current fragmentation of models and definitions hinders the accumulation of knowledge, making it difficult to compare findings across studies. Unified frameworks that integrate key concepts, variables, and mechanisms can establish a shared language for analyzing the complex interactions between human insights and AI attention mechanisms. Such theoretical grounding is indispensable not only for academic progress but also for translating insights into consistent and applicable practices.

Second, building upon these foundations, research should extend the empirical base across diverse contexts, sectors, and organizational settings. Standardized frameworks would provide common definitions and operationalizations, enabling systematic investigation of the dynamics of AI–human interplay. Expanding empirical coverage in this way is essential to identify recurring patterns, enhance comparability across studies, and increase the generalizability of results, thereby strengthening the evidence base and refining theoretical assumptions.

Finally, future studies should aim to broaden and deepen the recommendations for managerial practice (Chaturvedi et al., 2025). By combining empirical findings with robust conceptual models, scholars can generate actionable guidance that addresses concrete barriers to adoption and integration. Such insights would equip managers with tailored strategies to overcome trust, organizational, and ethical challenges, ensuring that AI–human collaboration fulfills its potential as both a driver of decision quality and a catalyst for organizational transformation.

References

Aal, E. (2025). 'The end user takes the final decision': AI and decision–communication in organisations. *Systems Research and Behavioral Science, 42*(2), 455–476. https://doi.org/10.1002/sres.3124

Akhunova, S., Tuychiyeva, O., Akhunova, M., & Tukhtasinova, D. (2024). *An innovative navigating system design along with AI tech integration for modern system implementation for business*. 2024 4th International Conference on Advance Computing and Innovative Technologies in Engineering ICACITE 2024 (pp. 462–467). https://doi.org/10.1109/ICACITE60783.2024.10616591

Baduna, M., & Hylving, L. (2023). *Dynamics of trust: Unpacking trust in human-AI collaboration in decision-making*. 29th Annual Americas Conference on Information Systems AMCIS 2023.

Boyacı, T., Canyakmaz, C., & de Véricourt, F. (2024). Human and machine: The impact of machine input on decision making under cognitive limitations. *Management Science, 70*(2), 1258–1275. https://doi.org/10.1287/mnsc.2023.4744

Carter, L., & Liu, D. (2025). How was my performance? Exploring the role of anchoring bias in AI-assisted decision making. *International Journal of Information Management, 82*. https://doi.org/10.1016/j.ijinfomgt.2025.102875

Chanda, A. K. (2024). Human judgment in artificial intelligence for business decision-making: An empirical study. *International Journal of Innovation Management, 28*(1–2). https://doi.org/10.1142/S136391962450004X

Chaturvedi, A., Yadav, N., & Dasgupta, M. (2025). Tech-driven transformation: Unravelling the role of artificial intelligence in shaping strategic decision-making. *International Journal of Human Computer Interaction*. https://doi.org/10.1080/10447318.2025.2456534

Choi, S., Kang, H., Kim, N., & Kim, J. (2025). How does artificial intelligence improve human decision-making? Evidence from the AI-powered Go program. *Strategic Management Journal*. https://doi.org/10.1002/smj.3694

Cooke, A., Smith, D., & Booth, A. (2012). Beyond PICO: The SPIDER tool for qualitative evidence synthesis. *Qualitative Health Research, 22*(10), 1435–1443. https://doi.org/10.1177/1049732312452938

Dellermann, D., Ebel, P., Söllner, M., & Leimeister, J. M. (2019). Hybrid intelligence. *Business & Information Systems Engineering, 61*(5), 637–643. https://doi.org/10.1007/s12599-019-00595-2

Glienke, M., Hartwich, N. J., & Antons, D. (2023). Working with AI: How Attitudes Shape Human-AI Collaboration. *ICIS 2023 Proceedings*, 12. https://aisel.aisnet.org/icis2023/hti/hti/12

Goel, P. K., & Mahur, L. S. (2025). Impact of generative AI on business analytics and decision making in service organizations. In *Generative AI for business analytics and strategic decision making in service industry* (pp. 65–88). IGI Global. https://doi.org/10.4018/979-8-3693-7026-1.ch003

Haesevoets, T., Dierckx, K., Van Hiel, A., & De Cremer, D. (2021). Human-machine collaboration in managerial decision making. *Computers in Human Behavior, 119*. https://doi.org/10.1016/j.chb.2021.106730

Herath Pathirannehelage, S., von Krogh, G., & Shrestha, Y. R. (2025). Design principles for artificial intelligence-augmented decision making: An action design research study. *European Journal of Information Systems, 34*(2), 207–229. https://doi.org/10.1080/0960085X.2024.2330402

Ines, J. C., Mirano, C. E., Vergara, J. A., Tolentino, M. Q., Cruz, J. C. D., Estabillo, R., & Madlambayan, A. M. (2024). *The role of AI in enhancing decision-making in small and medium enterprises (SMEs)*. 2024 2nd International Conference on Computing and Data Analytics ICCDA 2024 Proceedings. https://doi.org/10.1109/ICCDA64887.2024.10867356

Janhunen, E., Toivikko, T., Blomqvist, K., & Siemon, D. (2024). *Trust in digital human-AI team collaboration: A systematic review*. 30th Americas Conference on Information Systems AMCIS 2024.

Keding, C., & Meissner, P. (2021). Managerial overreliance on AI-augmented decision-making processes: How the use of AI-based advisory systems shapes choice behavior in R&D investment decisions. *Technological Forecasting and Social Change, 171*. https://doi.org/10.1016/j.techfore.2021.120970

Kheterpal, S., Chadha, A., & Kaur, K. (2024). Artificial intelligence in enhancing organisational performance: A thematic and factorial analysis. *Proceedings of the 5th International Conference on Smart Electronics and Communication ICOSEC 2024* (pp. 1634–1639). https://doi.org/10.1109/ICOSEC61587.2024.10722455

Klein, G., Moon, B., & Hoffman, R. R. (2007). Making sense of sensemaking: I. Alternative perspectives. *IEEE Intelligent Systems, 22*(4), 70–73.

Kotter, J. P. (1995). Why transformation efforts fail. *Harvard Business Review, 73*(2), 59–67.

Kotter, J. P. (2014). *Accelerate: Building strategic agility for a faster-moving world*. Harvard Business Review Press.

Lim, T. P., & Ravesangar, K. (2025). The integration of AI in performance appraisal: Balancing automation with human judgment. In *Artificial intelligence in peace, justice, and strong institutions* (pp. 321–351). IGI Global. https://doi.org/10.4018/979-8-3693-9395-6.ch015

Manoharan, G., Sharma, P., Chaudhary, V., Chatterjee Biswas, P., Sharma, M. K., & Lourens, M. (2024). *The future of work: Examining the impact of AI/ML on job roles, organizational structures, and talent management practices*. TQCEBT 2024 2nd IEEE International Conference on Trends in Quantum Computing and Emerging Business Technologies 2024. https://doi.org/10.1109/TQCEBT59414.2024.10545125

Masaeid, T. A., Alkhalidi, M. M., Ali, A. A. A. A., Almaazmi, S. M. G. A., & Alami, R. (2025). Artificial intelligence-augmented decision-making: Examining the interplay between machine learning algorithms and human judgment in organizational leadership. *Journal of Ecohumanism, 4*(1), 4683–4699. https://doi.org/10.62754/joe.v4i1.6364

Meyer, J. (2024). Doing Artificial Intelligence (AI): Algorithmic Decision Support as a Human Activity. *Decision, 11*(4), 481–492. https://doi.org/10.1037/dec0000241

Molina, D. A., Kharlov, V., & Chen, J.-S. (2024). *Towards effective human-AI collaboration in decision-making: A comprehensive review and conceptual framework*. PICMET 2024 2024 Portland International Conference on Management of Engineering and Technology Management in the Artificial Intelligence Era Proceedings. https://doi.org/10.23919/PICMET64035.2024.10653303

Mou, D., Cui, T., Holtta-Otto, K., Du, B., & Tong, J. (2024). *Effective stereotypical bias detection: The impact of human-AI collaboration modes on human reliance on AI*. ACIS 2024.

Neiroukh, S., Aljuhmani, H. Y., & Alnajdawi, S. (2024). *In the era of emerging technologies: Discovering the impact of artificial intelligence capabilities on timely decision-making and business performance*. 2024 ASU International Conference in Emerging Technologies for Sustainability and Intelligent Systems ICETSIS 2024 (pp. 866–871). https://doi.org/10.1109/ICETSIS61505.2024.10459356

Ngoc, T. N., & Elbanna, A. (2023). *Understanding human-AI augmentation in business and management context: A literature review*. ECIS 2023 Research Papers.

Okoli, C. (2015). A guide to conducting a standalone systematic literature review. *Communications of the Association for Information Systems, 37*(1), 879–910. https://doi.org/10.17705/1cais.03743

Page, M. J., McKenzie, J. E., Bossuyt, P. M., Boutron, I., Hoffmann, T. C., Mulrow, C. D., Shamseer, L., Tetzlaff, J. M., Akl, E. A., Brennan, S. E., Chou, R., Glanville, J., Grimshaw, J. M., Hróbjartsson, A., Lalu, M. M., Li, T., Loder, E. W., Mayo-Wilson, E., McDonald, S., et al. (2021). The PRISMA 2020 statement: An updated guideline for reporting systematic reviews. *BMJ, 372*, n71. https://doi.org/10.1136/bmj.n71

Ramos, I., & Barros, V. (2024). *The Interplay of human and AI attention in organizations*. ICIS 2024 TREOS.

Reddy, K. S., Kethan, M., Mahabub Basha, S., Singh, A., Kumar, P., & Ashalatha, D. (2024). *Ethical and legal implications of AI on business and employment: Privacy, bias, and accountability*. 2024 International Conference on Knowledge Engineering and Communication Systems Ickecs 2024. https://doi.org/10.1109/ICKECS61492.2024.10616875

Scarton, G., Formentini, M., & Romano, P. (2025). Automating quality control through an expert system. *Electronic Markets, 35*(1). https://doi.org/10.1007/s12525-025-00766-y

Schemmer, M., Hemmer, P., Nitsche, M., Kuhl, N., & Vossing, M. (2022). *A meta-analysis of the utility of explainable artificial intelligence in human-AI decision-making* (pp. 617–626). https://doi.org/10.1145/3514094.3534128

Sharma, R., & Reddy, B. (2024). *Strategic approaches to AI integration in organizations: Managing change and maximizing benefits*. 2024 4th Asian Conference on Innovation in Technology ASIANCON 2024. https://doi.org/10.1109/ASIANCON62057.2024.10838046

Steyvers, M., & Kumar, A. (2024). Three challenges for AI-assisted decision-making. *Perspectives on Psychological Science, 19*(5), 722–734. https://doi.org/10.1177/17456916231181102

Tabesh, P. (2022). Who's making the decisions? How managers can harness artificial intelligence and remain in charge. *Journal of Business Strategy, 43*(6), 373–380. https://doi.org/10.1108/JBS-05-2021-0090

Trunk, A., Birkel, H., & Hartmann, E. (2020). On the current state of combining human and artificial intelligence for strategic organizational decision making. *Business Research, 13*(3), 875–919. https://doi.org/10.1007/s40685-020-00133-x

Vom Brocke, J., Simons, A., Riemer, K., Niehaves, B., Plattfaut, R., & Cleven, A. (2015). Standing on the shoulders of giants: Challenges and recommendations of literature search in information systems research. *Communications of the association for information systems, 37*(1), 9. https://doi.org/10.17705/1cais.03709

Webster, J., & Watson, R. T. (2002). Analyzing the past to prepare for the future: Writing a literature review. *MIS Quarterly, 26*(2), xiii–xxiii.

Zhang, M., Xu, Y., & Wei, X. (2024). *AI-centered vs. human-centered: Exploring users' attitude toward AIGC in varying forms of human-AI collaboration*. PACIS 2024.

Designing for Intelligence Augmentation

Human-Centered AI Design and Implementation for Intelligence Augmentation

Can Kadir Oguz, Maurice Meyer, and Isabel Ramos

Declarations

- ChatGPT was used to improve the final quality of the text. ChatGPT was also used to identify the initial search strings for the articles to be included in the first phase of the literature review. The authors later refined these initial strings through successive adjustments and verification of the results. The authors reviewed and take full responsibility for the content of this chapter.

1 Introduction

In recent years, Artificial Intelligence (AI) has evolved from a largely theoretical concept into a pervasive technology that influences decision-making, creativity, and productivity. Within organizations, AI systems are increasingly integrated into workflows that support reasoning, pattern recognition, and problem-solving. This transformation has intensified debates on how human intelligence can be extended rather than replaced by intelligent systems, giving rise to the concept of Intelligence Augmentation (IAUG), the use of AI to enhance human thinking and action (Szczerbicki & Sanin, 2022).

Public discourse around AI is often shaped by dystopian imaginaries in which autonomous systems displace human agency and concentrate control in opaque infrastructures. Against this backdrop, Intelligence Augmentation offers an alternative trajectory in which AI extends, rather than replaces, human capabilities (Hegland, 2023). This vision builds on Engelbart's early work on "augmenting human intellect," which conceived computers as tools for amplifying human problem-solving and collective sense-making rather than simulating or superseding human cognition (Zhou et al., 2021). Recasting contemporary developments in

C. K. Oguz · M. Meyer
Department of Information Systems, University of Münster, Münster, Germany
e-mail: coguz@uni-muenster.de; mmeyer8@uni-muenster.de

I. Ramos (✉)
Department of Information Systems, University of Minho, Guimarães, Portugal
e-mail: iramos@dsi.uminho.pt

I. Ramos et al. (eds.), *Hybrid Attention in Organizations*, SpringerBriefs in Information Systems, https://doi.org/10.1007/978-3-032-30186-4_3

generative and predictive AI through this lens foregrounds augmentation as a socio-technical design choice rather than an inevitable outcome of technological progress.

Unlike automation, which seeks to substitute human judgment, IAUG emphasizes the creation of symbiotic relationships in which humans and machines leverage their respective strengths. AI contributes precision, scalability, and computational efficiency, while humans provide contextual understanding, ethical reasoning, and creativity. Together, these complementary capacities enable more effective responses to complex problems than either humans or machines could achieve alone.

The notion of Human-Centered Artificial Intelligence (HCAI) provides a framework for realizing this vision. It advocates designing AI systems that prioritize human agency, transparency, and trust while supporting decision-making and collaboration. However, despite the growing interest in HCAI and IAUG, the mechanisms through which these systems enhance human cognition and collective intelligence remain underexplored. Existing research often emphasizes technical performance or ethical considerations in isolation, leaving a gap in understanding how genuine augmentation of attention, reasoning, and judgment emerges from human–AI collaboration.

Addressing this gap requires a deeper examination of the socio-technical dynamics that shape IAUG. Questions about how attention is allocated, how meaning is co-constructed, and how responsibility is shared in hybrid systems are central to advancing both theory and practice. This paper responds to these challenges by systematically reviewing the literature to clarify the conceptual foundations of IAUG, identify key design principles, and assess implementation patterns. By doing so, it contributes to a more coherent understanding of how AI can be intentionally designed to extend human insight and strengthen organizational decision-making.

This chapter starts by outlining the systematic methodology developed in accordance with the PRISMA 2020 guidelines. It summarizes the comprehensive search strategy applied across major academic databases and the subsequent literature analysis procedures. The chapter then synthesizes findings from 21 primary studies, identifying the key design elements, challenges, and implementation patterns that characterize Human-Centered Artificial Intelligence for Intelligence Augmentation. The discussion then revolves around the interpretation of these results, illustrating how HCAI is applied in practice and examining the major barriers that constrain its effective implementation.

2 Research Methodology

This study employs a systematic literature review (SLR) to identify, evaluate, and synthesize the fragmented body of knowledge concerning how Human-Centered Artificial Intelligence is designed and implemented to support Intelligence Augmentation. Systematic reviews have become an essential methodological instrument in Information Systems research for producing cumulative, conceptually coherent insights in rapidly evolving domains. Following the PRISMA 2020 guidelines (Page et al., 2021), this review was conducted with an explicit commitment to transparency, replicability, and methodological rigor. PRISMA's structured approach enabled a traceable audit trail from search strategy formulation to final synthesis, ensuring that inclusion decisions, quality assessments, and thematic integrations were consistently documented and reproducible.

Guided by the overarching research question:

How is Human-Centered AI designed and implemented for Intelligence Augmentation?

the methodological process unfolded across four interrelated stages. First, a theoretically informed search strategy was developed to capture multidisciplinary scholarship across IS, HCI, and AI design. Second, studies were screened and selected according to pre-specified eligibility criteria, ensuring conceptual alignment with augmentation rather than automation. Third, data extraction and quality assurance procedures were implemented using dual independent coding and a harmonized bias-assessment protocol to enhance inter-rater reliability and mitigate selection bias. Finally, a concept-centric thematic synthesis was conducted to integrate insights across diverse empirical and conceptual contributions, allowing the review to surface core design logics, implementation patterns, and socio-technical challenges associated with HCAI for IAUG. This structured and rigorous approach ensures that the resulting synthesis offers a robust and theoretically grounded contribution to ongoing debates on human–AI collaboration within the Information Systems discipline.

2.1 Search Strategy

A comprehensive and structured search was conducted across four major academic databases—*Scopus*, *AIS eLibrary*, *Web of Science*, and the *ACM Digital Library*—to capture the multidisciplinary breadth of the topic across Information Systems, Computer Science, and Human–Computer Interaction.

The search strategy was informed by the SPICE framework (Setting, Perspective, Intervention, Comparison, Evaluation), ensuring alignment between the conceptual scope and the search queries. Keywords were organized accordingly.

Boolean combinations of the keywords in Table 1 were adapted to the specific syntax and field structures of each database. For each source, search strings were constructed using proximity operators and field restrictions (e.g., title, abstract, and keywords) to balance recall and precision. Truncation symbols (e.g., "organization*", "explainab*") and phrase searches (e.g., "intelligence augmentation", "human-centered AI") were systematically applied to capture relevant lexical variations while avoiding an unmanageable volume of irrelevant records. Database-specific constraints (such as maximum query length and supported Boolean

Table 1 Mapping of SPICE elements to search keywords and concepts

SPICE Element	Application to this review	Example keywords
Setting	Organizational and knowledge-work contexts where AI systems are implemented	"Organization*", "workplace*", "workflow", "decision-making"
Perspective	Human actors interacting with or affected by AI systems	"Human", "employee*", "user*", "knowledge worker*", "decision maker*"
Intervention	Human-Centered AI designed for Intelligence Augmentation	"Intelligence augmentation", "augmented intelligence", "human-centered AI", "human-in-the-loop", "AI-supported"
Evaluation	Reported impacts and performance dimensions	"Trust", "transparency", "explainab*", "efficiency", "ethical", "fairness", "accountability"

operators) were documented, and equivalent search logic was reconstructed where exact replication was not technically possible. The final queries were restricted to peer-reviewed journal articles and conference proceedings in English, within the 2020–2025 time frame.

Pilot testing in Scopus and AIS eLibrary was conducted to iteratively refine the search strings. Initial runs assessed the conceptual relevance and disciplinary fit of the top 30 retrieved articles per database, based on titles, abstracts, and keywords. This assessment surfaced additional recurring terms, such as "AI-supported decision-making," "workflow augmentation," and "human-in-the-loop systems," which were incorporated into the search strings as complementary synonyms or related constructs. At each iteration, the sample of retrieved records was re-examined to ensure that precision improved (fewer clearly irrelevant articles) without compromising coverage of diverse IAUG-related contexts. The refinement process concluded when further adjustments no longer yielded substantively new conceptual variants, indicating a satisfactory balance between sensitivity and specificity of the search.

To complement the database searches and mitigate the risk of omitting influential or emergent work, forward and backward snowballing procedures were applied (Wohlin, 2014). Backward snowballing involved screening the reference lists of all provisionally included studies to identify earlier foundational or conceptually aligned publications. Forward snowballing was conducted using Google Scholar to retrieve articles that cited the included studies, thereby capturing more recent and interdisciplinary contributions. Each candidate identified through snowballing was subjected to the same eligibility criteria as database-derived records, and duplicates were removed using reference-management software. This iterative process, repeated until no new relevant studies emerged in subsequent snowballing rounds, enhanced the completeness of the corpus and ensured that emerging, cross-disciplinary work on Human-Centered AI and Intelligence Augmentation was adequately represented.

2.2 *Eligibility Criteria*

To ensure the inclusion of high-quality and relevant studies, explicit inclusion and exclusion criteria were defined *a priori*. The inclusion criteria specified that only peer-reviewed journal articles and conference papers published in English between 2020 and 2025 would be considered. This temporal window was chosen to capture the most recent developments in Human-Centered AI and Intelligence Augmentation, particularly those emerging after the diffusion of large language models and generative AI systems. Restricting the corpus to peer-reviewed English-language publications further ensured that all selected studies would be accessible for systematic synthesis and subject to established scholarly quality controls.

Conceptually, eligible studies were required to focus on Intelligence Augmentation, Human-Centered AI design, or human-in-the-loop systems that explicitly aim to augment, rather than replace human capabilities in organizational or decision-making contexts. Such studies directly address the central focus of the review: how AI systems are designed to enhance human cognition and decision-making quality rather than fully automate these processes. Including this body of work enables the identification of mechanisms, design patterns, and evaluation metrics specifically relevant to collaborative human–AI intelligence.

In parallel, several exclusion criteria were applied to maintain conceptual coherence and methodological rigor. First, research focused exclusively on full automation without human involvement was excluded to avoid conflating augmentation with automation and to keep the analysis centered on hybrid human–AI configurations where shared control and interpretive agency are present. Second, purely technical or algorithmic studies that omit discussion of human collaboration were removed, as they typically lack theoretical or empirical insight into the social, cognitive, or organizational dimensions of systems designed for augmented intelligence. Finally, non-peer-reviewed sources (such as white papers, blogs, and preprints) and studies for which the full text was inaccessible were excluded. This decision ensured reliance on verifiable, publicly accessible scientific outputs and minimized potential biases stemming from non-validated or commercially driven materials.

2.3 *Study Selection Process*

The study selection followed the multi-stage PRISMA screening procedure (Fig. 1). Search results from all databases were exported to Zotero for centralized reference management and systematic duplicate removal. Of the 52 records initially retrieved, *47 unique studies* remained after deduplication and were carried forward to the screening phase.

Two independent reviewers then screened titles and abstracts against the predefined eligibility criteria, carefully assessing each record for conceptual alignment

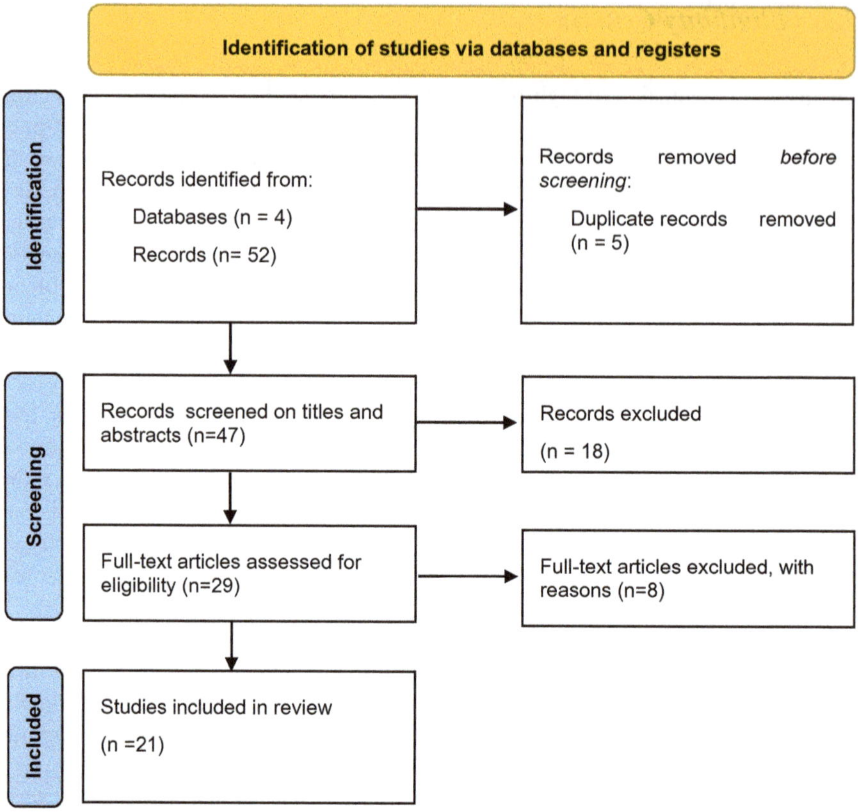

Fig. 1 Overview of the selection process [Adapted from Page et al. (2021)]

with Human-Centered AI and Intelligence Augmentation, as well as basic methodological relevance. This stage reduced the pool to 29 potentially relevant papers. The full texts of these studies were subsequently retrieved and subjected to an in-depth assessment using a standardized evaluation template, which captured key dimensions such as HCAI focus, IA focus, design principles, human-in-the-loop role, underlying frameworks or models, and reported challenges.

Throughout the process, discrepancies and borderline cases were resolved through joint review sessions. These discussions were supported by comparison notes and justification logs, ensuring that inclusion and exclusion decisions were transparent and well documented. This iterative consensus-building approach strengthened inter-rater reliability and reinforced the methodological rigor of the review, ultimately resulting in a final corpus of *21 primary studies*.

2.4 Data Extraction and Quality Assurance

Two reviewers independently extracted data to minimize human bias, with inconsistencies resolved through consensus discussions. A structured data extraction template, implemented in a shared spreadsheet, was used to ensure comparability across studies. The template captured, among other fields, paper ID, authors, outlet, domain or context, HCAI focus, IAUG focus, reported design principles, the human-in-the-loop role, proposed frameworks or models, and documented challenges. This schema enabled a concept-centric synthesis by aligning heterogeneous studies around common analytical dimensions rather than treating each contribution as an isolated case.

To assess the robustness of the included studies, a risk-of-bias assessment was conducted. Given the methodological heterogeneity of HCAI and IAUG research, a harmonized quality-assessment approach was preferred over standard appraisal tools (e.g., CASP, AMSTAR). Three bias-control mechanisms were applied:

1. *Selection Bias Mitigation*—Dual independent screening using predefined criteria.
2. *Source Credibility Verification*—Restricting inclusion to peer-reviewed works from established databases.
3. *Contextual Diversity Check*—Ensuring representation across varied domains (e.g., healthcare, finance, customer service, data science) to enhance generalizability.

Together, these three mechanisms confirmed the robustness of the review process. Selection Bias Mitigation reduced arbitrary exclusions and strengthened inter-rater reliability, while Source Credibility Verification ensured that all included studies met peer-reviewed standards from reputable databases. The Contextual Diversity Check demonstrated that the final corpus represented multiple domains, enhancing generalizability and revealing underexplored contexts. Collectively, these measures proved effective in increasing transparency, methodological rigor, and confidence in the synthesized evidence.

2.5 Synthesis of Evidence

The synthesis followed a concept-centric thematic analysis (Tranfield et al., 2003; Webster & Watson, 2002). Extracted material was coded into initial categories that captured HCAI philosophies and principles, IA design approaches, frameworks and models, and human-in-the-loop configurations.

These categories were iteratively refined using Miro-based visual mapping to trace conceptual linkages, overlaps, and tensions across studies. This integrative process enabled the identification of recurring design logics and implementation challenges that define Human-Centered AI for Intelligence Augmentation.

This integrative procedure crystallized a set of recurrent design logics and cross-cutting implementation challenges that define Human-Centered AI for Intelligence Augmentation. It yielded a structured synthesis of the 21 primary studies, integrating core design elements, theoretical foundations, and empirical insights presented in the next section.

3 Thematic Synthesis of Human-Centered Intelligence Augmentation

This section synthesizes the findings of the SLR into three interrelated thematic pillars that collectively articulate the core principles and practices underlying HCAI in the context of IAUG. First, the literature demonstrates a clear shift toward designing AI systems around human values and interpretive capacities, with the explicit aim of enhancing, rather than replacing, human cognition. This orientation foregrounds the importance of contextual understanding, sense-making, and user empowerment as foundational elements of augmentation.

Second, the reviewed studies consistently highlight the structural embedding of human oversight through human-in-the-loop mechanisms. These mechanisms ensure that users retain meaningful agency and accountability in decision processes, while also enabling iterative feedback that supports mutual learning between humans and AI systems.

Third, ethical principles, most notably transparency, fairness, and related constructs of explainability and accountability, are increasingly treated as integral design requirements rather than supplementary considerations. These ethical commitments are presented as essential for fostering trust, mitigating risk, and sustaining long-term human–AI collaboration.

Taken together, these thematic pillars portray HCAI as a socio-technical configuration that enables the deliberate augmentation of human intelligence. They illustrate how effective IAUG emerges from a careful balance of computational automation with interpretability, human control, and moral responsibility, ultimately positioning human–AI partnership as a coherent and viable paradigm for organizational intelligence.

3.1 AI Systems Designed Around Human Values and Interpretive Capacities

Across the reviewed studies, IAUG is consistently distinguished from full automation by its human-centric orientation. Rather than delegating decision-making to autonomous systems, IAUG focuses on extending human perceptual, analytical, and creative abilities (Shneiderman, 2020; Zhou et al., 2021; Schmager et al., 2025).

The central objective is to align technological affordances with human interpretive processes and contextual judgment, ensuring that AI supports rather than supplants cognition. Shneiderman (2020) describes this approach as a design philosophy that "enables people to see, think, create, and act in extraordinary ways," emphasizing empowerment, agency, and accountability. Similarly, Zhou et al. (2021) define IAUG as enhancing human decision-making quality through context-sensitive assistance, in which AI provides computational depth while humans retain semantic and ethical framing.

Empirical work reinforces that effective IAUG design begins with a deep understanding of user goals, contexts, and cognitive models. Schmager et al. (2025) show that when design processes explicitly integrate user perspectives and domain knowledge, the resulting systems promote situational awareness and foster trust. Conversely, automation without interpretive alignment often produces cognitive misfits, AI outputs that are formally correct yet contextually meaningless to the user. Studies of managerial, medical, and legal applications repeatedly demonstrate that IAUG's success depends on whether its reasoning and representations remain legible and actionable within human sense-making frameworks (Henriksen & Blond, 2023; Lee & Cha, 2023). In this way, IAUG reframes design priorities so that computational performance alone is no longer sufficient and human interpretability becomes the primary benchmark of system value.

This emphasis on human-aligned design marks a conceptual transition from "artificial intelligence" to "augmented intelligence," a paradigm where interpretability, context sensitivity, and human values are core design constraints. The reviewed studies converge on the view that augmentation succeeds only when the machine's analytical reach is balanced by the human's contextual understanding, creating a dynamic partnership between data-driven inference and meaning-making.

3.2 *Human Oversight Structurally Embedded Through Human-in-the-Loop Mechanisms*

A defining practice across the literature is the structural embedding of human oversight and intervention throughout the AI lifecycle. Human-in-the-loop configurations ensure that people remain active participants in data curation, model supervision, and decision refinement, thereby aligning system behavior with human judgment (Shneiderman, 2020; Grønsund & Aanestad, 2020). This participatory design ethos addresses long-standing concerns over autonomy, control, and explainability by keeping humans involved in every critical loop of information processing. For example, clinicians routinely validate AI-generated diagnostic suggestions before these insights are incorporated into patient care decisions.

Evidence from applied studies shows that human-in-the-loop architectures enhance both performance and accountability. In operational domains such as healthcare and finance, humans intervene at decision-critical junctures to validate AI outputs or handle ambiguity (Pieper & Gleasure, 2025). In creative or strategic contexts, collaboration becomes iterative. Humans and machines co-generate alternatives, and through mutual feedback cycles, refine outputs that neither could achieve independently (Gerber et al., 2020; Harborth & Kümpers, 2022). This dynamic interplay enables systems to learn from user corrections while users learn from AI-generated insights, producing what Gerber et al. (2020) call *symbiotic intelligence*.

However, several studies caution that the benefits of human oversight are contingent on clear role definition and cognitive load management. Poorly designed interfaces can shift users from empowered collaborators to passive monitors, reproducing the "ironies of automation" where supervision becomes more cognitively demanding than direct control. Henriksen and Blond (2023) and Pieper and Gleasure (2025) stress that successful IAUG design requires distributed agency. The system should handle computation-intensive subtasks, while humans contribute context, ethical evaluation, and reflective learning. When this division of labor is explicit and well-supported, human-in-the-loop mechanisms foster a mutually adaptive partnership that sustains attention, trust, and shared responsibility.

Overall, embedding human oversight not only mitigates risks of opacity and over-automation but also institutionalizes a feedback ecology in which human and artificial attentions continuously calibrate each other. This structural coupling of human and machine agency forms the operational backbone of Intelligence Augmentation.

3.3 Ethical Principles as Design Imperatives

The third thematic pillar underscores that ethical principles, particularly transparency, fairness, accountability, and trustworthiness, are increasingly treated as *intrinsic design criteria* rather than peripheral considerations. HCAI frameworks converge on the view that IAUG can succeed only when its operations are intelligible, justifiable, and aligned with social values (Zhou et al., 2021; Lee & Cha, 2023; Henriksen & Blond, 2023).

Explainability and transparency function as the primary mediators of trust between humans and AI systems. Lee and Cha (2023) demonstrate that users' confidence in AI decisions grows when models provide interpretable rationales, enabling contestability and oversight. Herm et al. (2023) and Zhou et al. (2023) further observe that transparency mechanisms, such as traceable decision paths or interpretable visualizations, reduce perceived opacity, helping users build accurate mental models of system reasoning. Fairness and accountability complement this by addressing the socio-ethical dimension of augmentation and by requiring that IAUG systems uphold equitable treatment while clearly delineating responsibility within human–AI collaborations (Henriksen & Blond, 2023; Paul et al., 2022).

Collectively, these ethical design imperatives extend the goals of HCAI beyond usability toward moral and epistemic alignment. Fairness auditing, bias mitigation, and responsibility tracing are not optional safeguards but central mechanisms that preserve legitimacy and user agency. As Schmager et al. (2025) argue, treating ethics as a modular "add-on" invites systemic fragility, whereas integrating ethical principles into design architectures produces more resilient and trustworthy systems. Importantly, the reviewed studies indicate that these values must be operationalized through explainable models, transparent interfaces, and clear accountability protocols, rather than confined to high-level policy statements. When properly enacted, ethical design imperatives transform IAUG from a technological innovation into a normatively grounded socio-technical system.

3.4 Conceptual Frameworks for Human-Centered Intelligence Augmentation

A complementary strand of the literature proposes conceptual frameworks that formalize how Human-Centered AI can be harnessed for Intelligence Augmentation. Shneiderman's two-dimensional HCAI framework positions systems along axes of automation and human control, highlighting design spaces in which high automation can coexist with strong human agency and oversight (Shneiderman, 2020). Building on this, Zhou et al. articulate a 6W-H model and an IA ecosystem framework that specify why, what, how, who, where, and when AI should augment human actors, linking design principles such as simplification, interpretability, human-centeredness, and ethics to specific stakeholder roles and contexts (Zhou et al., 2021, 2023). Other contributions, such as Gerber et al.'s human–machine symbiosis framework and Harborth and Kümpers' task-typology for IA solutions, emphasize complementarity and co-adaptation by classifying how different kinds of human work (procedural, analytical-creative, social) can be supported by distinct augmentation logics. Finally, integrative HCAI frameworks (e.g., Schmager et al., 2025) foreground governance, traceability, and stakeholder engagement as preconditions for making these design propositions actionable. Taken together, these models provide a scaffolding for IAUG research and practice by translating abstract human-centered values into configurable design spaces and governance mechanisms.

Across the reviewed frameworks, the ethical principles of transparency, explainability, trust, fairness, ethics, and accountability define the normative core of HCAI for IAUG. Rather than functioning as standalone checkboxes, these principles operate as an interdependent set in which transparency and explainability support calibrated trust, fairness and ethics anchor system behavior in distributive and procedural justice, and accountability clarifies how responsibilities are allocated and made enforceable in hybrid human–AI configurations.

3.5 Summary of Insights

Synthesizing across these thematic pillars, the literature portrays Intelligence Augmentation as a *transformative configuration of human–machine collaboration*. The guiding philosophy is not efficiency through automation but enhanced cognition through cooperation. AI systems designed around human interpretive capacities preserve meaning and agency; structurally embedded human oversight ensures adaptability and accountability; and ethics-by-design safeguards fairness, transparency, and trust. Together, these dimensions converge on a vision of HCAI where augmentation is achieved through mutual adaptation between human and artificial intelligences.

In addressing the research question—*How is Human-Centered AI designed and implemented for Intelligence Augmentation?*—the synthesis reveals that effective IAUG requires an integration of cognitive, organizational, and ethical design logics. It is this triangulation among interpretability, oversight, and ethics that distinguishes IAUG from traditional automation and positions it as a viable paradigm for human-AI symbiosis. The collective evidence suggests that when these elements cohere, IAUG not only enhances individual and organizational performance but also reinforces the fundamental principle that intelligence, human or artificial, attains its fullest potential through collaboration grounded in human values.

4 Challenges in Organizational Implementation of Intelligence Augmentation

Implementing IAUG in organizational contexts is subject to multiple barriers that affect its conceptual clarity, ethical grounding, operational reliability, and workforce integration. These barriers must be carefully addressed to enable IAUG to move beyond experimental deployments and realize its potential as a paradigm for human–AI collaboration.

4.1 Conceptual Ambiguities

A persistent barrier concerns the lack of consensus on how Intelligence Augmentation (IAUG) and Human-Centered AI (HCAI) should be conceptually defined. Scholars have repeatedly noted that this absence of conceptual clarity undermines consistent application across studies and domains (Schmager et al., 2025). Terms such as HCAI are often invoked as rhetorical markers to signal ethical intent, yet they are not always accompanied by concrete design practices that operationalize human-centered principles. As a result, the terminology becomes diffuse and risks losing analytical value. This definitional fragmentation hinders the accumulation of cumulative knowledge and obstructs efforts to develop standardized frameworks that could guide theory building and empirical evaluation. Without greater precision in how IAUG and HCAI are delineated, organizations may implement systems that appear "human-centered" in name but lack the genuine augmentative features required for meaningful human–AI collaboration.

4.2 *Ethical and Societal Concerns*

Ethical and societal concerns constitute a significant and persistent challenge in the adoption of Intelligence Augmentation (IAUG). AI systems often replicate and, in some cases, amplify social biases embedded in training data, creating the risk of unfair or discriminatory outcomes in sensitive organizational processes (Zhou et al., 2021). Importantly, such biases may remain latent even under careful oversight, thereby perpetuating inequities in decision-making and undermining the legitimacy of human–AI collaboration. Beyond bias, IAUG technologies must contend with the difficulty of operationalizing context-dependent values such as justice, autonomy, and dignity in a consistent and actionable manner (Henriksen & Blond, 2023; Schmager et al., 2025). These normative constructs are inherently situated and can vary across domains, cultures, and organizational settings, complicating their translation into system-level requirements. Moreover, the substantial computational resources demanded by contemporary AI models raise sustainability concerns, as the environmental and energy-related costs may conflict with organizational commitments to responsibility and long-term technological stewardship (Schmager et al., 2025). Taken together, these ethical and societal complexities highlight the need for IAUG frameworks that embed normative principles directly into design and evaluation processes, rather than treating ethics as an external or downstream consideration.

4.3 *Human–AI Conflict Dynamics*

Human–AI collaboration inevitably generates points of tension when machine outputs diverge from human judgment. These discrepancies, rooted in fundamentally different modes of observation, interpretation, and action, can undermine trust and reduce decision quality when left unaddressed (Wen & Khan, 2024). Importantly, such divergences are frequently misinterpreted as system errors or human mistakes, rather than as manifestations of distinct cognitive models operating in parallel. This misattribution obscures the underlying sources of conflict and can prompt users to override, ignore, or abandon AI recommendations, thereby negating the intended benefits of augmentation. Although Wen and Khan (2024) propose risk-based models to anticipate and quantify these conflict dynamics, empirical evidence indicates that organizations rarely implement systematic mechanisms to identify, mediate, and learn from them. Sustaining IAUG in practice, therefore, requires proactive conflict-resolution strategies that preserve trust, support reciprocal adaptation, and reinforce the conditions for effective human–AI symbiosis.

4.4 Workforce and Role Transformation

The workforce and role transformation required by IAUG presents a substantial barrier to its effective implementation. IAUG reshapes established professional roles by redistributing expertise between humans and machines, which can inadvertently lead to employee deskilling when opportunities for independent judgment and complex problem-solving diminish (Zhou et al., 2023). Over time, sustained reliance on AI tools may erode critical thinking and reduce human proficiency in tasks that previously relied heavily on experiential knowledge. At the same time, employees must develop new competencies, particularly the ability to interpret, scrutinize, and contextualize AI-generated outputs within their domain-specific workflows (Schmager et al., 2025). These adjustments demand cognitive, procedural, and cultural adaptation. When IAUG systems are introduced through top-down directives without sufficient training, consultation, or role redesign, employees often experience uncertainty, resistance, and disengagement (Henriksen & Blond, 2023). Consequently, successful IAUG adoption requires intentional workforce reskilling efforts, participatory implementation strategies, and organizational cultures that emphasize augmentation as a mechanism for empowerment rather than displacement.

5 Applications and Implementations of Human-Centered Intelligence Augmentation

Practical implementations of HCAI reveal how the core design principles of Intelligence Augmentation (IAUG) translate into real-world contexts. Across domains, from healthcare and finance to education and public services, successful initiatives demonstrate systems intentionally aligned with human values, structured for human oversight, and ethically grounded in transparency and fairness.

The reviewed evidence suggests that IAUG is largely scope-agnostic. Wherever human–AI collaboration can outperform either humans or machines alone, augmentative configurations become a viable design option (Schmager et al., 2025; Zhou et al., 2023). This generality explains the growing presence of IAUG systems across healthcare, finance, consulting, human resources, customer service (e.g., Lin et al., 2024), education, and public-sector decision-making.

5.1 *AI Systems Designed Around Human Values and Interpretive Capacities*

Healthcare applications exemplify IAUG systems that strengthen professional judgment rather than automate it. Radiology tools such as the *AI-Rad Companion Chest X-ray* automatically identify frequent pathologies but present results as interpretable cues to assist, not replace, clinicians (Pieper & Gleasure, 2025). These systems enable doctors to focus on complex diagnostic reasoning and patient communication, reflecting the principle that AI should amplify, not substitute, human expertise (Hassani et al., 2020; Zhou et al., 2021). Similarly, an AI-supported pen-like camera used in brain cancer surgery predicted malignancy with over 90% accuracy, expanding surgeons' precision while keeping decision authority with the human (Paul et al., 2022). Such designs embed medical knowledge, context, and professional ethics directly into the interaction, demonstrating alignment with human interpretive capacities.

In consulting, augmented-reality smart glasses provide real-time market data during client meetings, allowing consultants to integrate computational insights into situational interpretation (Harborth & Kümpers, 2022). This mirrors IAUG's human-centered ethos, in which AI enhances situational awareness while leaving meaning-making to the human expert.

5.2 *Human Oversight Structurally Embedded Through Human-in-the-Loop Mechanisms*

Many implementations explicitly embed oversight through *human-in-the-Loop* configurations. In venture capital analysis, AI rapidly evaluates investment opportunities, but human experts perform a "big-picture" review, applying contextual and ethical judgment before final decisions (Jarrahi, 2018; Hassani & Silva, 2023). Likewise, in financial services, human-in-the-loop approaches safeguard critical reasoning. For instance, the CleverLoan system in a German bank automated small-loan decisions but inadvertently deskilled advisors by excluding them from decision processes (Mayer et al., 2020). Later refinements reintroduced human validation steps, illustrating how active oversight preserves both expertise and trust.

In human resources, embedding humans in recruitment loops ensures fairness and transparency when algorithms screen applicants. By allowing human auditors to review and adjust automated recommendations, organizations align efficiency goals with ethical accountability (Lee & Cha, 2023; Paul et al., 2022). Across these examples, oversight mechanisms maintain a balance of automation and control (Shneiderman, 2020).

5.3 *Ethical Principles as Design Imperatives*

Ethical imperatives drive many IAUG applications, especially where algorithmic opacity risks fairness and accountability. In the public sector, predictive systems used for urban planning or policing expose the tension between efficiency and equity. While such tools can aid decision-making, their "black-box" nature raises concerns about discrimination and over-reliance (Zhou et al., 2023; Paul et al., 2022). Embedding transparency features, such as explainable interfaces or auditable logs, addresses these issues and fosters public trust.

In healthcare and finance alike, continuous bias monitoring and accountability structures are integrated as part of the system lifecycle (Henriksen & Blond, 2023; Schmager et al., 2025). These implementations demonstrate that ethics cannot remain peripheral. Fairness auditing and interpretability must be operationalized within the very architecture of IAUG systems.

5.4 *Integrative Perspective*

Across domains, these examples do more than illustrate isolated best practices; they reveal a shared socio-technical logic that conditions the success of Intelligence Augmentation. Effective IAUG emerges when technological architectures are explicitly aligned with human interpretive values, when oversight is institutionalized through meaningful human-in-the-loop roles, and when ethical safeguards are treated as design constraints rather than afterthoughts. Under these conditions, systems deployed for diagnosis, investment analysis, consulting, or public decision-making do not merely increase efficiency; they reconfigure how expertise, responsibility, and trust are distributed between humans and machines. In this integrative perspective, IAUG's distinctive contribution lies in its ability to extend human insight while maintaining fairness, transparency, and accountability as non-negotiable anchors of system design, governance, and everyday use.

6 Conclusion

This systematic literature review set out to answer: *How is Human-Centered AI designed and implemented for Intelligence Augmentation?* By analyzing 21 primary studies, our synthesis demonstrates a paradigm shift from automation to augmentation, where AI is not a substitute for human cognition but a partner in amplifying it. Three central insights define this emerging paradigm. First, AI systems are increasingly designed around human values and interpretive capacities, ensuring that technological outputs remain meaningful and actionable within human sense-making frameworks. Second, human oversight is structurally embedded through human-in-the-loop mechanisms, safeguarding agency, accountability, and adaptive learning. Third, ethical principles such as transparency, fairness, and trustworthiness are not peripheral but foundational design imperatives. Together, these insights establish IAUG as a socio-technical configuration in which computational precision and human judgment are deliberately integrated.

6.1 Theoretical Implications

Theoretically, this SLR clarifies long-standing conceptual ambiguities by disentangling Intelligence Augmentation from both full automation and general notions of "ethical AI." Our synthesis aligns divergent frameworks (e.g., Shneiderman's Human-Centered AI, Zhou et al.'s design principles) around shared commitments to interpretability, human-centeredness, and ethics. By mapping how human–AI symbiosis is theorized across disciplines, we provide a more coherent conceptual foundation for future research. Importantly, this study highlights that IAUG should be seen not merely as a technological trend but as a distinct paradigm of organizational cognition that reframes the boundaries of decision-making, attention, and responsibility in hybrid human–AI systems.

6.2 Practical Implications

For practice, this review translates abstract principles into actionable design and management guidance. Developers and organizational leaders can treat interpretability, oversight, and ethics as a three-part design checklist: (1) ensure that outputs align with human interpretive capacities; (2) embed structured human-in-the-loop oversight at critical junctures of data curation, model supervision, and decision-making; and (3) operationalize fairness, transparency, and accountability through concrete design mechanisms such as explainable interfaces and audit trails. Case evidence from healthcare, finance, and HR demonstrates both benefits and pitfalls, showing that while IAUG can enhance precision, efficiency, and fairness, it may also create risks such as deskilling, bias reinforcement, and unresolved human–AI conflicts. Organizations should therefore combine IAUG deployment with workforce reskilling initiatives, participatory design practices, and explicit conflict-resolution protocols to sustain trust and long-term effectiveness.

6.3 Limitations

Despite methodological rigor following PRISMA guidelines, this SLR has limitations. The review is confined to four major databases and the 2020–2025 time window, which may omit earlier or non-indexed contributions. Moreover, as the field evolves rapidly, particularly with generative AI, the findings represent a snapshot rather than an endpoint. Conceptual ambiguities persist around definitions of IAUG and HCAI, underscoring the need for more precise theorization and empirical validation.

6.4 Future Research

Future research should address three urgent directions. First, longitudinal case studies are required to trace how IAUG systems reshape organizational roles, skills, and cultures over time, as only sustained observation can reveal whether augmentation strengthens human expertise or gradually erodes it through dependence and deskilling. Second, greater attention should be devoted to the dynamics of human–AI conflict, developing adaptive mechanisms for reconciliation rather than override, because unresolved divergences between human judgment and machine output threaten not only system effectiveness but also user trust and long-term adoption. Third, the sustainability dimension of IAUG, particularly the energy demands of advanced models, warrants systematic integration into design and policy debates, since the environmental costs of large-scale AI may ultimately constrain the scalability and societal legitimacy of augmentation initiatives.

References

Gerber, A., Derckx, P., Döppner, D. A., & Schoder, D. (2020). Conceptualization of the human–machine symbiosis: A literature review. In *Proceedings of the 53rd Hawaii International Conference on System Sciences (HICSS)* (pp. 1–10). University of Hawai'i at Mānoa, Honolulu, HI. https://doi.org/10.24251/HICSS.2020.036

Grønsund, T., & Aanestad, M. (2020). Augmenting the algorithm: Emerging human-in-the-loop work configurations. *Journal of Strategic Information Systems, 29*(2), 101614. https://doi.org/10.1016/j.jsis.2020.101614

Harborth, D., & Kümpers, K. (2022). Intelligence augmentation: Rethinking the future of work by leveraging human performance and abilities. *Virtual Reality, 26*(4), 849–870. https://doi.org/10.1007/s10055-021-00590-7

Hassani, H., & Silva, E. S. (2023). The role of ChatGPT in data science: How AI-assisted conversational interfaces are revolutionizing the field. *Big Data and Cognitive Computing, 7*(2), 62. https://doi.org/10.3390/bdcc7020062

Hassani, H., Silva, E. S., Unger, S., TajMazinani, M., & Mac Feely, S. (2020). Artificial intelligence (AI) or intelligence augmentation (IA): What is the future? *AI, 1*(2), 143–155. https://doi.org/10.3390/ai1020008

Hegland, F. (2023). IA, not only AI. In *Proceedings of the 34th ACM Conference on Hypertext and Social Media (HT '23)* (pp. 1–5). ACM.

Henriksen, A., & Blond, L. (2023). Executive-centered AI? Designing predictive systems for the public sector. *Social Studies of Science, 53*(5), 738–760. https://doi.org/10.1177/03063127231163756

Herm, L.-V., Heinrich, K., Wanner, J., & Janiesch, C. (2023). Stop ordering machine learning algorithms by their explainability! A user-centered investigation of performance and explainability. *International Journal of Information Management, 71*, 102538. https://doi.org/10.1016/j.ijinfomgt.2022.102538

Jarrahi, M. H. (2018). Artificial intelligence and the future of work: Human-AI symbiosis in organizational decision making. *Business Horizons, 61*(4), 577–586. https://doi.org/10.1016/j.bushor.2018.03.007

Lee, C., & Cha, K. (2023). FAT-CAT—Explainability and augmentation for an AI system: A case study on AI recruitment-system adoption. *International Journal of Human–Computer Studies, 171*, 102976. https://doi.org/10.1016/j.ijhcs.2022.102976

Lin, X., Wang, X., Shao, B., & Taylor, J. (2024). How chatbots augment human intelligence in customer services: A mixed-methods study. *Journal of Management Information Systems, 41*(4), 1016–1041. https://doi.org/10.1080/07421222.2024.2415773

Mayer, A.-S., Strich, F., & Fiedler, M. (2020). Unintended consequences of introducing AI systems for decision making. MIS Quarterly. *Executive, 19*(4), 239–254.

Page, M. J., McKenzie, J. E., Bossuyt, P. M., Boutron, I., Hoffmann, T. C., Mulrow, C. D., Shamseer, L., Tetzlaff, J. M., Akl, E. A., Brennan, S. E., Chou, R., Glanville, J., Grimshaw, J. M., Hróbjartsson, A., Lalu, M. M., Li, T., Loder, E. W., Mayo-Wilson, E., McDonald, S., et al. (2021). The PRISMA 2020 statement: An updated guideline for reporting systematic reviews. *BMJ, 372*, n71. https://doi.org/10.1136/bmj.n71

Paul, S., Yuan, L., Jain, H. K., Robert, L. P., Spohrer, J., & Lifshitz-Assaf, H. (2022). Intelligence augmentation: Human factors in AI and future of work. *AIS Transactions on Human–Computer Interaction, 14*(3), 426–445. https://doi.org/10.17705/1thci.00174

Pieper, M., & Gleasure, R. (2025). How AI helps to compile human intelligence: An empirical study of emerging augmented intelligence for medical image scanning. *Information Systems Journal, 35*(5), 1399–1421. https://doi.org/10.1111/isj.12585

Schmager, S., Pappas, I. O., & Vassilakopoulou, P. (2025). Understanding human-centred AI: A review of its defining elements and a research agenda. *Behaviour & Information Technology, 44*(15), 3771–3810. https://doi.org/10.1080/0144929X.2024.2448719

Shneiderman, B. (2020). Human-centered artificial intelligence: Three fresh ideas. *AIS Transactions on Human–Computer Interaction, 12*(3), 109–124. https://doi.org/10.17705/1thci.00131

Szczerbicki, E., & Sanin, C. (2022). Experience-based intelligence augmentation with decisional DNA: Upcoming direction. *Procedia Computer Science, 207*, 522–531. https://doi.org/10.1016/j.procs.2022.09.107

Tranfield, D., Denyer, D., & Smart, P. (2003). Towards a methodology for developing evidence-informed management knowledge by means of systematic review. *British Journal of Management, 14*(3), 207–222. https://doi.org/10.1111/1467-8551.00375

Webster, J., & Watson, R. T. (2002). Analyzing the past to prepare for the future: Writing a literature review. *MIS Quarterly, 26*(2), xiii–xxiii.

Wen, H., & Khan, F. (2024). A risk-based model for human–artificial intelligence conflict resolution in process systems. *Digital Chemical Engineering, 13*, 100194. https://doi.org/10.1016/j.dche.2024.100194

Wohlin, C. (2014). Guidelines for snowballing in systematic literature studies and a replication in software engineering. *Proceedings of the 18th International Conference on Evaluation and Assessment in Software Engineering* (pp. 1–10). ACM. https://doi.org/10.1145/2601248.2601268

Zhou, L., Paul, S., Demirkan, H., Yuan, L., Spohrer, J., Zhou, M., & Basu, J. (2021). Intelligence augmentation: Towards building human–machine symbiotic relationship. *AIS Transactions on Human–Computer Interaction, 13*(2), 243–264. https://doi.org/10.17705/1thci.00149

Zhou, L., Rudin, C., Gombolay, M., Spohrer, J., Zhou, M., & Paul, S. (2023). From artificial intelligence (AI) to intelligence augmentation (IA): Design principles, potential risks, and emerging issues. *AIS Transactions on Human–Computer Interaction, 15*(1), 111–135. https://doi.org/10.17705/1thci.00185

Synthesis and Outlook

Hybrid Attention as an Organizational Capability

Isabel Ramos, Katrin Bergener, and Armin Stein

1 Integrating Learning, Decision-Making, and Intelligence Augmentation

The preceding analyses of AI in organizational learning, decision-making, and intelligence augmentation reveal a unifying thread, namely that attention is the mechanism that links data-driven technologies with human knowledge processes. Taken together, the literature shows that AI attention mechanisms can convert raw data flows into meaningful feedback, which in turn drives organizational learning and improvement. By selectively focusing on relevant information, AI systems transform feedback from a one-way transfer into a reflexive dialogue between humans and machines, enabling continuous knowledge refinement and shared understanding. In other words, attention provides the connective tissue by which data become information, information becomes organizational knowledge, and knowledge guides action. This attentional linking from data to sensemaking is what allows organizations to learn from complex data in real time and to respond intelligently.

A closer look at each domain illustrates how hybrid attention operates in practice. In the organizational learning context, AI's attention mechanisms enhance feedback-driven learning cycles. Research indicates that Generative AI (GenAI)

I. Ramos (✉)
Department of Information Systems, University of Minho, Guimarães, Portugal
e-mail: iramos@dsi.uminho.pt

K. Bergener
Department of Information Systems (ERCIS), University of Münster, Münster, Germany
e-mail: katrin.bergener@uni-muenster.de

A. Stein
Institute of Information Systems, University of Münster, Münster, Germany
e-mail: armin.stein@uni-muenster.de

I. Ramos et al. (eds.), *Hybrid Attention in Organizations*, SpringerBriefs in Information Systems, https://doi.org/10.1007/978-3-032-30186-4_4

attention can filter informational noise and highlight salient knowledge, helping organizations overcome information overload and focus on learning what matters. Such systems function as *attentional agents* within knowledge management processes, structuring how knowledge is noticed, retained, and shared across the firm. Human and AI attention thereby interact to form reflexive learning loops, as humans train AI models with feedback and, in turn, algorithmic outputs reshape human understanding and sensemaking. This co-evolutionary feedback process enables more adaptive and context-aware organizational learning outcomes than either humans or AI could achieve alone. The result is a shift in knowledge management paradigms, from merely accumulating information to fostering context-aware, selective, and feedback-driven learning that continuously aligns data insights with organizational knowledge needs.

In organizational decision-making, a hybrid attention approach similarly enhances the quality and timeliness of decisions. AI attention mechanisms excel at scanning vast, complex data environments and foregrounding the most salient signals, thus helping decision-makers not miss critical patterns in big data. Empirical studies show that AI can improve decision accuracy and speed by filtering out irrelevant information and presenting actionable insights to human managers. Meanwhile, human decision-makers contribute indispensable contextual judgment, intuition, and ethical reasoning to interpret AI outputs and vet their appropriateness. Rather than replace human insight, AI augments it. Technology handles computational complexity and pattern recognition at scale, while people apply experience-based sensemaking to ensure decisions are sensible and morally sound. This complementary division of labor has been found to increase decision effectiveness under the right conditions. For example, organizations achieve more timely, accurate, and accountable decisions when AI's machine precision is deliberately orchestrated with human wisdom. The synergy between AI attention and human attention, however, depends on organizational factors like trust, integration, and oversight, themes that will be discussed further in Sect. 3. When managed well, AI-augmented attention yields decisions that are better informed by data without losing the benefit of human discernment.

In the domain of intelligence augmentation (IAUG), the emphasis is on designing AI systems that *amplify* human cognitive capabilities rather than automating tasks outright. This perspective underscores a fundamental shift "from automation to augmentation," whereby AI becomes a partner to human cognition instead of a substitute. A human-centered AI design philosophy deliberately aligns AI system behavior with human cognitive strengths and limitations. For instance, interfaces are crafted to present AI outputs in human-interpretable form, and workflows are set up to include human-in-the-loop oversight at critical junctures. The systematic review of human-centered AI design for augmentation in chapter "Human-Centered AI Design and Implementation for Intelligence Augmentation" identified three core design logics: (1) ensuring AI outputs remain meaningful within human sensemaking frameworks, (2) embedding structured human oversight to safeguard agency and accountability, and (3) making ethical principles like transparency and fairness foundational in system design. These design principles confirm that effective augmentation requires more than raw algorithmic power; it requires socio-technical alignment so that AI amplifies human understanding, creativity, and decision-making rather than eclipsing them. In practice, organizations have found that intelligence augmentation can improve decision quality, innovation, and fairness, but only when systems are built to complement human interpretive capacities and not to operate as black-boxes. Thus, human-centered design is key to harnessing AI's attentional capabilities for *intelligence augmentation*, ensuring that humans remain in control of how attention is directed and applied.

Hybrid attention can now be conceptualized as a unifying meta-capability that links these domains (learning, decision-making, and augmentation) into a coherent strategic function. At its core, hybrid attention is the organizational ability to coordinate learning and deciding across levels and functions by managing attentional resources. It enables a firm to dynamically allocate focus, from raw data capture to insight generation, to knowledge dissemination, to responsive action. In this sense, hybrid attention acts as a linking mechanism from data to informed action. It connects the data-processing prowess of AI with the meaning-making faculties of humans, ensuring that signals detected by machines translate into shared knowledge and then into decisions or interventions. This capability is higher order because it governs other processes. For example, it governs which information will feed organizational learning and which options will be considered in decision-making. By integrating the attention-based view (ABV) of the firm with the knowledge-based view, we can see hybrid attention as an organizational competency to manage *what* the organization pays attention to, *how* learning is focused, and *where* decision-makers direct their efforts. This goes beyond any individual tool or person; it is an emergent property of the human–AI collaboration within the firm's structures and culture. Therefore, hybrid attention is a meta-capability to orchestrate collective attention (both human and machine) in alignment with strategic goals, thereby enhancing the organization's ability to learn continuously and make intelligent, timely decisions in a complex environment.

2 Hybrid Attention Ecosystems: Human, Artificial, and Organizational Levels

Understanding hybrid attention as an organizational phenomenon requires a multi-level perspective encompassing the micro (individual human), meso (AI system), and macro (organizational) levels. Figure 1 illustrates this ecosystem of attention, wherein human cognition, artificial attention mechanisms, and organizational structures are interlinked. At the micro-level, we consider how individual people attend to information, make sense of it, and share meaning. The meso-level comprises the AI systems and algorithms that allocate attention to data (for instance, transformer models identifying relevant inputs). The macro-level involves the organizational context, its structures, routines, and norms that channel collective attention and govern what the organization notices or ignores. Rather than operating in isolation,

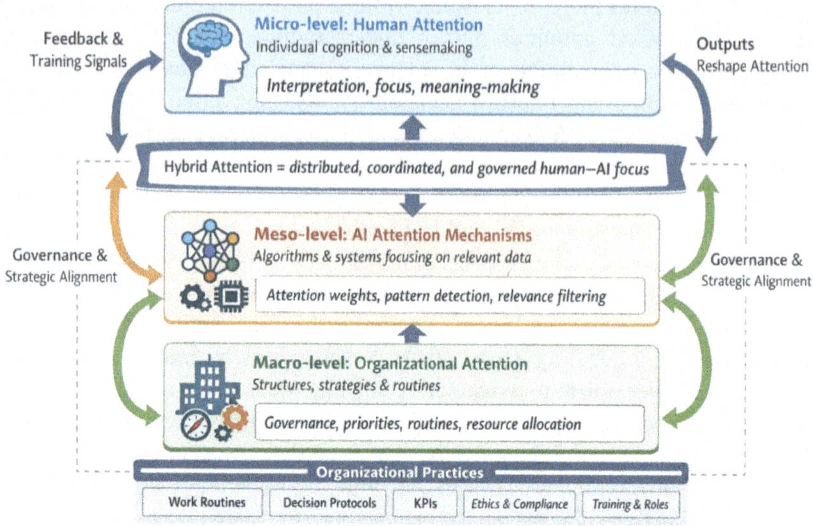

Fig. 1 Multi-level hybrid attention ecosystem

these levels continuously interact and shape one another, forming an integrated hybrid attention system. This socio-technical ecosystem view highlights that effective organizational attention emerges from coordination across all levels. The patterns of individual attention, the design of AI attentional mechanisms, and the organizational policies that guide and stabilize attention in the long run.

At the micro (human) level, attention involves individual cognitive processes of noticing, interpreting, and prioritizing information. Humans bring qualitative judgment and contextual common sense that remain essential even in data-rich environments. For example, managers rely on experiential knowledge and intuition to discern which data patterns are meaningful in light of the organization's context. Human attention is also guided by values and ethics, as people can question whether an insight is not only technically significant but also *appropriate* to act on. This level includes the rich processes of sensemaking by which individuals and teams construct meaning from ambiguous information. It is inherently flexible and creative. Humans can reframe problems, generate novel insights, and notice anomalies that fall outside predefined criteria. However, human attentional capacity is limited; people are prone to cognitive biases and information overload. This is why the micro-level benefits from support at the meso-level. AI systems can help by sifting through volumes of data and drawing human attention to areas of potential importance.

At the meso-level (AI system), attention is manifested in the algorithmic filtering and highlighting of information. Modern AI models implement attention mechanisms that enable them to weigh the relevance of different inputs, essentially telling the system "where to look" when analyzing data. Within organizational applications, these mechanisms serve as amplifiers and filters for human analysts. They rapidly process large datasets, detect patterns or anomalies, and bring forward the salient signals amid noise. For instance, a diagnostic AI might flag unusual trends in real-time operational data that a human manager should consider, or a recommendation system might personalize information retrieval for an employee by learning what content is most relevant to their tasks. The meso-level therefore extends the reach and scale of organizational attention; it ensures that potentially important data points (which humans alone might overlook due to volume or complexity) are given due consideration. Crucially, AI attention is not static; these systems can be updated through feedback. When humans provide corrections or additional inputs (for example, telling a system that a flagged item is a false alarm or highlighting a new category of concern), the AI can adjust its attention parameters. This adaptive feedback loop means the AI's focus evolves over time in response to human judgment. Thus, the meso-level is characterized by dynamic learning. The AI's attentional policies co-evolve with human guidance, reflecting a form of machine learning aligned with organizational knowledge.

At the macro (organizational) level, attention is shaped by the firm's structures, culture, and strategic priorities. The attention-based view of the firm (Ocasio, 1997) posits that what an organization does is a function of what issues and answers it pays attention to. Organizational attention is allocated through mechanisms like formal structures, routines, and prioritization frameworks (strategic plans, objectives, and key results). These structures serve to distribute and stabilize collective attention. They signal to members what the organization deems important, and they routinize the processing of information (e.g., regular KPI reviews focus attention on certain metrics). In a hybrid attention scenario, the macro-level context must also encompass AI systems as new actors in the attention structure. Whereas traditional organizations allocate attention through human roles and communication channels, contemporary organizations integrate AI agents that automatically scan and prioritize information. The result is that organizational routines increasingly include human–AI interactions. For example, a monthly business review might include insights generated by an AI analytics tool alongside human reports. Organizational governance needs to ensure that these AI contributions align with strategic goals (so that the AI is "looking at" what matters for the strategy) and adhere to the organization's values (so that the way information is filtered by AI is acceptable and ethical). At the macro-level, attention is coordinated and legitimized; top management and governance bodies set the agenda for attention (what gets resources and review), and they institutionalize practices that maintain an effective balance between exploration and exploitation of knowledge. Over time, stable patterns of hybrid attention (e.g., regular use of certain AI tools and defined human oversight) become part of the organizational memory and culture.

Critically, these three levels are interdependent and jointly constitute the *hybrid attention ecosystem*. Attentional processes at one level influence and are influenced by those at other levels as the arrows in Fig. 1 illustrate. For instance, if an AI system at the meso-level starts highlighting a new market trend, human managers at the micro-level may shift their attention to investigate it further, potentially leading the organization at the macro-level to adapt its strategic focus. Conversely, if top management decides a certain issue (like cybersecurity) is strategically crucial, they may invest in AI monitoring tools (meso) and mandate employees (micro) to prioritize that issue, thereby reallocating attention throughout the system. This dynamic can be described as co-evolution. Humans adapt their ways of working as they learn to trust and use AI outputs, and AI systems adapt through ongoing human feedback and changing organizational objectives. Research has noted that such recursive human–AI configurations expand the traditional boundaries of organizational learning and decision-making by creating new feedback loops. Moreover, attention itself becomes an object of design and management. Rather than assuming human attention as a given, organizations now design socio-technical systems to actively manage attention flows.

A multi-level hybrid attention perspective also emphasizes how attention is coordinated and stabilized across levels. Coordination refers to aligning the focus of humans and AI in complementary ways (so that, for example, AI is not directing attention to trivial issues, and humans are not ignoring critical algorithmic signals). Stabilization refers to developing reliable routines and norms such that hybrid attention processes are repeatable and trusted within the organization. One way this happens is through the creation of shared frameworks and interfaces that allow humans and AI to understand each other's signals. For example, explainable AI interfaces at the meso-level can present reasons for an AI's recommendation, enabling a human at the micro-level to comprehend and respond appropriately. This fosters a shared attentional frame and trust. Likewise, organizational policies at the macro-level (such as requiring human sign-off for certain AI-triggered decisions) create a stable division of *attentional labor* that everyone understands. Over time, these mechanisms lead to an attentional equilibrium where the volatility of human–AI interaction (especially in early adoption phases) is smoothed into accepted practice. Scholars note that attentional processes are embedded in socio-material practices, not just in individual minds. In hybrid settings, this means practices like regular cross-functional AI review meetings, update sessions to recalibrate AI models with human input, and governance reviews of AI system performance are all part of embedding hybrid attention into the fabric of organizational life. By grounding attention in practice and governance, the organization can ensure that the collective focusing power of humans and AI is sustained and directed toward its goals.

Thus, a hybrid attention ecosystem spans micro human cognition, meso AI mechanism, and macro organizational context, each contributing distinct capabilities to the organization's overall attentional capacity. The *distribution* of attention across these levels allows organizations to be simultaneously detail-oriented (via AI's granular analysis) and big-picture in sensemaking (via human judgment and strategic oversight). The coordination across levels, achieved through feedback loops and governance, ensures that human and AI attention reinforce rather than conflict with each other, producing a sum greater than the parts. And the stabilization via institutionalized practices and roles secures the benefits of hybrid attention over time, preventing chaos or drift. Hybrid attention as an organizational capability thus resides not in any single level, but in the *configuration and alignment* of all three levels into an adaptive attentional system. This system represents a new kind of socio-technical partnership, one where machine precision and human wisdom are orchestrated deliberately to optimize organizational outcomes. The next sections will delve into how such orchestration is governed responsibly (Sect. 3) and how scholars and practitioners can further advance the understanding of hybrid attention (Sect. 4).

3 Governance, Ethics, and Responsible AI

While hybrid attention offers powerful opportunities, it also raises critical governance and ethical challenges. Ensuring that human and AI attention work together effectively requires more than technical integration, it demands attentional governance. Deliberate management of who or what decides what is salient, how signals are balanced, and how biases and blind spots are mitigated. The literature across organizational learning, decision-making, and HCAI design converges on a key point: over-reliance on AI without appropriate oversight is dangerous. If organizations cede too much decision power to AI recommendations, they risk undermining human agency and accountability, reinforcing biases, and creating blind spots in sensemaking. In a hybrid attention system, there must therefore be clear guidelines about the respective roles of humans and AI in focusing attention and making judgments, i.e., a governance framework that preserves human responsibility and meaningful control.

One major concern is the risk of attentional biases and narrowing introduced or amplified by AI systems. AI attention mechanisms are data-driven and may systematically favor patterns present in historical data, potentially overlooking "weak signals" or novel information that fall outside past trends. This can lead to attentional narrowing, where the organization's focus becomes too myopic. For example, only targeting well-known customer segments because the AI's training data highlights those, while ignoring emerging markets or outlier events. Furthermore, biases in training data can skew what the AI deems relevant, causing certain viewpoints (often those of minority groups or unconventional ideas) to be filtered out. Chapter "AI Attention Mechanisms Enhancing Organizational Learning" highlights that studies have observed that generative AI in knowledge management might inadvertently reinforce existing knowledge biases and even reduce human collaboration if not carefully integrated. To combat this, governance must ensure diversity of input and perspective in the hybrid attention system. This could involve periodically auditing AI outputs for bias, diversifying the data the AI is trained on, and having humans deliberately inject alternative perspectives into the decision process. Transparency is vital. If the AI's criteria for relevance are opaque, it's difficult for humans to detect bias or correct the system's focus. Thus, implementing explainable AI techniques and making the AI's attention (what it focused on to reach a conclusion) visible to human reviewers is an important ethical safeguard.

Another interrelated challenge is deskilling or the erosion of human attentional skills. If employees come to overly rely on AI to tell them where to look and what to think, their own capacity for critical thinking and situational awareness may deteriorate. There is evidence that while AI augmentation can boost performance, it may also lead to user complacency or skill atrophy if human roles are reduced to simply accepting AI outputs. This is why responsible hybrid attention designs insist on keeping humans in-the-loop in meaningful ways. Governance policies should clarify that AI recommendations are advisory and that humans have a duty to stay engaged, cross-check, and override when necessary. Regular training and reskilling programs can help maintain human expertise. Employees should be trained not just in how to use AI tools, but also in critical thinking skills to interrogate AI outputs. Some organizations establish rotation programs where staff periodically perform tasks without AI assistance to keep their skills sharp and to better understand the AI's role. Overall, preserving human attentional capacity is both an ethical and practical imperative. Ethically, because individuals should retain autonomy and mastery over their work; practically, because human intuition and creativity are sources of long-term organizational adaptability that no static algorithm can replace.

A fundamental aspect of governance is clarifying accountability in hybrid decision systems. When AI and human attention jointly determine what is acted upon, who is responsible if something goes wrong? Organizations must avoid the trap of the "many hands" problem where responsibility becomes so diffuse that accountability is diluted. Effective governance frameworks assign clear decision rights and escalation paths. For example, a policy might state that AI can flag issues and even suggest actions, but a human manager must sign off on any critical decision, thereby the manager retains accountability. Some companies formalize roles such as an AI curator or AI ethics officer who is accountable for how the AI system directs attention and whether it aligns with company policy (Laine et al., 2024; Papagiannidis et al., 2023; Schneider et al., 2023). The research emphasizes that preserving human oversight and responsibility is crucial. AI should be viewed as a tool supporting human decision-makers, not an autonomous agent that absolves humans of decision consequences. In practice, this means instituting governance committees or review boards for AI initiatives, similar to risk management committees, that periodically review how AI is used in decision-making, investigate any failures or near-misses, and ensure lessons are learned. A culture of accountability also entails that employees are encouraged to question AI outputs and are protected (not penalized) when they identify errors or biases. This fosters active human engagement and prevents over-reliance.

Trust and transparency are enabling conditions for any hybrid attention arrangement to function effectively. Users must trust the AI's contributions, but that trust should be calibrated (i.e., neither blind faith nor undue skepticism). Achieving calibrated trust requires explainability. People need to understand why the AI is highlighting certain information or making certain recommendations. Therefore, organizations should prioritize AI systems that can provide interpretable reasons or visualizations of their attention focus. For instance, attention heatmaps or natural language explanations of an AI model's output can be provided to analysts, so they see not just *what* the AI recommends but *why*. Transparency also extends to clearly communicating the role of AI in workflows. If employees know exactly which steps of a process involve AI influence, they are better prepared to monitor and question those steps. Empirical findings suggest that trust in AI is strongly linked to perceptions of transparency and procedural fairness in how AI-driven decisions are made (see chapter "AI-Augmented Attention in Organizational Decision-Making"). Thus, ethical governance calls for "glass box" AI (as opposed to black-box), wherein the attentional logic of the system is as open to examination as feasible. Additionally, building trust involves iterative validation. Early successes where AI's attentional suggestions lead to good outcomes should be publicized within the organization, and failures should be openly analyzed to improve the system and training. Over time, a record of reliable performance, coupled with continued human oversight, will cultivate an environment of trust where humans and AI can each play to their strengths.

Bringing these threads together is the concept of attentional governance, a governance approach specifically focused on managing attention in hybrid human–AI systems. Attentional governance entails setting policies and mechanisms for deciding what gets attention and how. Concretely, this involves aligning the AI's algorithmic focus with the organization's strategic priorities and values, rather than leaving it to purely data-driven criteria. For example, if innovation is a strategic goal, governance might ensure the AI doesn't only reinforce past knowledge but also surfaces contrarian or novel ideas (preserving those "weak signals" that could be tomorrow's big opportunities). It also means establishing rules for balancing competing signals, deciding when efficiency should trump thoroughness or vice versa. In a flood of data, attention is a zero-sum game, as focusing on one thing means ignoring another. Attentional governance provides a framework for those trade-offs. One principle might be *attentional diversity*: ensuring a portfolio of attention where core issues get continuous focus but peripheral vision is maintained. Another principle is *rotation and escalation*: rotating focal areas periodically and having escalation paths for signals that the AI flags as anomalous (so they are not lost in a queue). Importantly, attentional governance also addresses ethical dimensions. It asks not only "are we paying attention to the right things for our business?" but also "are we doing so in a way that is fair, legal, and aligned with our societal responsibilities?". Questions of who gets to decide salience touch on power dynamics. For instance, if an AI prioritizes efficiency, does that undervalue employee well-being? Governance bodies should include diverse stakeholders (management, technical experts, front-line workers, possibly even external or customer representatives) to democratize the definition of what is salient. As one study suggests, organizations should design mechanisms so that automated attention does not *marginalize minority viewpoints or novel insights* that might hold future value (see chapter "AI Attention Mechanisms Enhancing Organizational Learning"). This might be operationalized by requiring human review of cases where the AI's recommendation is to ignore an outlier, or by maintaining channels for employees to bring up issues that the AI might have missed.

Finally, we must consider the broader ethical principle of human-centeredness in hybrid attention governance. The ultimate goal is not just effective information processing, but to ensure that the technology serves human purposes and upholds human values. This means governance frameworks should explicitly include fairness, accountability, transparency, and ethics as part of how attentional systems are evaluated and managed. Responsible AI guidelines should be extended to cover attention allocation (e.g., "We will be transparent about how our AI systems prioritize information" or "We will hold human decision-makers accountable for oversight of AI recommendations"). Embedding such principles into policies, training, and system design creates an environment where hybrid attention is practiced conscientiously. As a concrete step, some organizations are implementing audit trails for attention, logs of what recommendations the AI made and how humans responded, to be reviewed for bias or errors. Others are developing dashboard indicators of hybrid performance, for instance, measuring how often human overrides happen, or tracking diversity of sources the AI draws from, which can signal whether the attentional system is balanced or veering into problematic territory. By proactively addressing over-reliance, bias, deskilling, accountability, and transparency, organizations can create a *responsible hybrid attention system*, one that not only achieves performance gains but does so in a trustworthy, fair, and human-aligned manner.

4 Toward a Research Agenda on Hybrid Attention

As hybrid attention is a relatively new conceptual domain, there are rich opportunities for future research to deepen theoretical understanding, gather empirical evidence, and develop practical solutions. Building on the insights of this volume, we propose a forward-looking research agenda with several key avenues, each addressing different facets of hybrid attention. Below, we outline these avenues and highlight open research questions for each:

- *Theoretical Integration and Development*: There is a need to develop unified conceptual frameworks that integrate perspectives from the attention-based view (ABV), knowledge-based view (KBV), organizational learning, and human–AI collaboration theories. Current literature is fragmented. Researchers use varied models and terminology to discuss similar phenomena, hindering cumulative knowledge. A concerted effort to build coherent theory of hybrid attention is needed. What might such a theory include? One element could be formalizing the concept of hybrid attention as a meta-capability, perhaps drawing on dynamic capabilities theory to explain how organizations develop and deploy this capacity over time. Another element is articulating the mechanisms linking micro-, meso-, and macro-levels. For example, theoretical models that describe how individual attention routines and AI algorithms interact under different organizational structures. Open questions include: *How can we conceptually model the co-adaptation of human and AI attention?* and *What are the key constructs (e.g., "attentional alignment," "feedback elasticity," "attentional diversity") that explain variance in organizational outcomes?* Addressing these questions would likely involve synthesizing ideas from cognitive science, information systems, and organizational theory into an integrated framework. By aligning divergent conceptual lenses (e.g., human-centric AI design principles and classic organizational behavior theory), scholars can provide a shared language and set of constructs for hybrid attention. This theoretical foundation would not only clarify ambiguities (such as distinguishing hybrid attention from related concepts), but also position hybrid attention within the broader context of organizational cognition and collective intelligence.

- *Multi-Level and Longitudinal Empirical Research*: Empirical studies on hybrid attention should expand in scope and depth to validate and refine theoretical ideas. First, multi-level research designs are essential. Since hybrid attention phenomena span individuals, technologies, and organizations, studies that collect data at and link across these levels (for example, combining individual cognitive measures, AI system logs, and organizational performance metrics) are needed to capture the full picture. Second, longitudinal studies and experiments are particularly valuable to observe how hybrid attention capabilities develop or deteriorate over time. For instance, a longitudinal field study might track a company adopting an AI decision support tool over several years, examining how employees' trust and skills evolve, how the AI's recommendations change with continued feedback, and what long-term impact on decision quality is observed. Such studies can answer questions like: *Does sustained use of AI attention tools lead to improved human expertise (through learning) or to deskilling over time?* and *How do organizations successfully scale hybrid attention from pilot projects to enterprise-wide capabilities?* Additionally, comparative studies across different contexts (industries, cultures, task types) would help identify contingencies (e.g., hybrid attention might function differently in a high-reliability context like healthcare vs. an agile context like tech startups). Cross-sectional surveys and case studies could map the landscape of practice: *What patterns of human–AI attention collaboration exist in organizations today?* and *Which factors (e.g., organizational culture, nature of task, type of AI model) most strongly influence success or failure of hybrid attention initiatives?* Empirical research should also employ mixed methods. Quantitative measures (for decision accuracy, learning rates, etc.) can be paired with qualitative insights (from interviews, observations of how people make sense of AI outputs). By extending the empirical base across diverse settings and methods, we can begin to identify general principles as well as context-specific nuances of hybrid attention dynamics.
- *Design Science and Intervention Research*: Given the applied nature of hybrid attention, design-oriented research will be crucial to test and refine how we implement hybrid attention systems in practice. This involves both the technical design of AI tools and the organizational design of processes and roles. Scholars and practitioners can use design science research methods to create and evaluate prototypes of hybrid attention support systems. For example, new dashboard interfaces that visualize what the AI is focusing on to help users calibrate their attention, or interactive AI assistants that can engage in dialogue with users to jointly decide where to investigate further. Experimentation in real organizational settings (action research or pilot implementations) can yield insights on

what design features best foster effective human–AI attentional collaboration. For instance, research could ask: *How might an "attention dashboard" be designed to alert managers when either human or AI might be neglecting a critical issue?* or *What kind of explanation interface most improves human understanding of AI attention outputs in complex analytical tasks?* On the organizational process side, intervention studies could explore new management and teamwork practices for hybrid attention. One idea is to develop training programs specifically aimed at "attentional skills" in the age of AI, teaching employees how to work alongside AI to scan and interpret information. Another is designing governance interventions such as checklists or protocols (as suggested by the managerial implications in chapter "Human-Centered AI Design and Implementation for Intelligence Augmentation") that guide teams through incorporating AI input while maintaining human judgment. Researchers might partner with organizations to implement such interventions and measure outcomes (e.g., changes in decision quality, user satisfaction, knowledge sharing rates). Design science questions include: *What socio-technical configurations (combination of tool features and work practices) lead to the most synergistic human–AI attention allocation?* and *How can we design organizational routines that institutionalize learning from AI feedback while avoiding automation complacency?* Ultimately, this line of inquiry aims to produce actionable design principles and artifacts that organizations can adopt, bridging the gap between theoretical benefits of hybrid attention and practical reality.

- *Ethical, Governance, and Policy Inquiry*: As hybrid attention blurs the lines between human and machine agency in organizational sensemaking, it raises profound ethical and policy questions that merit dedicated research. Future studies should delve into the normative dimensions of hybrid attention: for instance, how power dynamics are affected when algorithms gatekeep information. One question is: *How do we ensure equitable attention in organizations—that AI doesn't inadvertently silence minority voices or unconventional ideas?* This links to the earlier point of attentional governance but from a normative angle: What ethical frameworks or regulations might be needed? Another crucial area is accountability and legal responsibility in AI-augmented decisions. Research could explore legal theory or policy analysis to ask: *Should there be formal regulations requiring human "attentional oversight" for AI systems in high-stakes domains (similar to how some industries mandate human oversight of automated systems)?* and *What kind of audit standards could be developed to assess bias or fairness in an organization's hybrid attention processes?* There is also the dimension of privacy. If AI is monitoring employees' activities to decide what information to push to whom, how do we balance efficiency with privacy rights? Moreover, the future of work and labor emerges as an ethical theme. As AI takes over certain attentional tasks, what are the implications for job design and employee well-being? Will employees feel less engaged or, conversely, more empowered to do creative work? Ethnographic and critical research could shed light on these human impacts, ensuring that the march toward hybrid intelligence keeps human dignity and agency front and center. Additionally, cross-cultural research might investigate how cultural differences affect trust in AI and willingness to rely on algorithmic attention. This could inform more culturally sensitive implementations of hybrid systems. Finally, an often-overlooked aspect is the sustainability of attention technologies. Advanced AI models (e.g., large language models driving attention mechanisms) consume significant energy and resources. A forward-looking question is: *How sustainable are hybrid attention solutions, and can they be designed to be both environmentally and socially sustainable?* Addressing these ethical and governance questions will likely require interdisciplinary approaches, bringing together IS scholars, ethicists, legal experts, and sociologists. The answers will help formulate guidelines and frameworks that ensure hybrid attention is not only effective but also responsible and aligned with societal values.

In summary, a robust research agenda on hybrid attention spans theoretical, empirical, design, and ethical inquiries. It calls for integrated theory-building, diverse and longitudinal empirical studies, inventive design science experiments, and critical ethical/policy analysis. Pursuing these directions will advance a cumulative research program that links the technical design of attention mechanisms with their human and institutional consequences. The resulting knowledge can enrich both information systems theory and organizational practice, guiding us toward hybrid attention systems that are intelligent, trustworthy, and human-centered.

5 Final Reflections

Hybrid attention as an organizational capability heralds a transformative shift in how organizations make sense of their environment and act upon it. By fusing human cognitive strengths with artificial intelligence capabilities, organizations can achieve a form of collective intelligence that is greater than the sum of its parts. This has profound implications for organizational sensemaking. Traditionally, sensemaking in organizations, the process by which groups interpret complex, ambiguous information, has been limited by human cognitive constraints. Now, with AI's attentional power, organizations can process and interpret far more information, yet do so in a way that retains human intuition and values. Hybrid attention systems enable what we might call augmented sensemaking, which is the ability to detect subtle patterns in data and contextualize them within the organization's narrative and strategy. When human analysts and AI systems engage in a continuous feedback loop, the organization becomes more adept at spotting emerging threats and opportunities, questioning assumptions, and adapting its understanding. This contributes to a more resilient and learning-oriented organization, one that can navigate complexity with both analytical rigor and interpretive savvy. In effect, hybrid attention broadens the cognitive bandwidth of the organization; more signals can be perceived and correctly understood, without overwhelming the human decision-makers, because the AI helps manage the flood of data.

For managerial practice, the rise of hybrid attention means that managers must evolve from being sole decision-makers to being orchestrators of human–AI collaboration. The managerial role increasingly involves attentional leadership, deciding where to direct the combined focus of teams and intelligent machines. Managers will need to cultivate new skills, such as the ability to critically evaluate AI insights, to coach their teams in effective use of AI tools, and to design workflows that integrate AI input at the right points. They must also remain vigilant about the risks, ensuring, for example, that an overzealous algorithm doesn't lead the team astray or that important insights from frontline employees aren't dismissed just because the AI didn't flag them. Leading in a hybrid attention context thus requires a balance of trust and skepticism: trust in the tools' capabilities and skepticism that maintains healthy oversight. Additionally, organizations may see new specialized roles emerging (or expanding) in managerial ranks, including data curators, AI ethicists, human–AI interaction managers, all focused on managing the interface between machine-generated signals and human decision processes. On a strategic level, executives will likely spend more time on questions of attentional strategy. In a world of information abundance, choosing *what not to focus on* can be as important as what to focus on. Hybrid attention capabilities will inform these choices by providing better intelligence, but executives will still impart the vision and values that determine ultimate priorities. Companies that excel at hybrid attention are likely to have a competitive edge in decision speed and accuracy, innovation, and adaptability. Therefore, it becomes a managerial imperative to invest not only in AI technologies, but also in the organizational capital (training, culture, process design) that makes those technologies effective contributors to collective attention.

The broader future of work and human agency is also shaped by the adoption of hybrid attention systems. Optimistically, intelligence augmentation offers a vision of the future where AI empowers workers rather than displacing them. Routine, monotonous attentional tasks (monitoring dashboards, sifting through raw data logs) can be offloaded to AI, freeing humans to concentrate on creative, strategic, and interpersonal aspects of work. In such a future, work could become more fulfilling. Employees act on synthesized insights and engage in problem-solving with the support of their AI "colleagues," rather than drowning in data drudgery. Human agency in this scenario is enhanced because people have better tools to inform their judgment and can achieve outcomes previously out of reach. However, realizing this future requires conscious effort to implement AI in a human-centered way. If done poorly, there is a risk that AI could in fact diminish agency. For instance, if employees are reduced to blindly following AI recommendations or if surveillance-oriented AI systems start dictating workers' every move. The balance of agency must be carefully managed. Humans should always feel that they are the ones setting goals and making the final calls, with AI serving as an advisor and assistant. Organizations that strike this balance will likely see high employee acceptance of AI and even enthusiasm, as technology is viewed as an augmentation of their expertise and not a threat to their autonomy. On a societal level, fostering human agency in the age of AI is crucial for avoiding dystopian outcomes. Hybrid attention presents a narrative counter to automation-driven job loss. It is, rather, about job transformation and skill elevation. The hope is that as mundane attentional labor is automated, new opportunities for human creativity and higher-order thinking flourish. Education and continuous learning will be key. Tomorrow's workforce should be trained in collaboration skills with AI, critical thinking, and adaptability, so that they can leverage hybrid attention tools to expand their own capabilities.

Throughout this book, we have seen a consistent shift from automation to augmentation; a reimagining of AI not as a replacement for human intelligence, but as a complement that amplifies human potential. Instead of viewing AI as an autonomous decision-maker, the chapters in this volume have portrayed it as part of a joint cognitive system, participating in organizational attention alongside humans. This represents a profound change in mindset, from focusing on individual human cognition to embracing a notion of collective hybrid intelligence. In collective hybrid intelligence, problem-solving and sensemaking are accomplished by a team of diverse intelligences working in concert—human minds with their rich understanding and values, and machine minds with their speed and breadth of analysis. The central message underscored by our synthesis is that by designing and managing AI for augmentation rather than automation, organizations can enhance their performance while retaining human judgment and values at the core of their processes. Hybrid attention is the linchpin of this transformation. It is through the coordinated focus of humans and AI that data is turned not just into decisions, but into decisions that are contextually smart, ethically informed, and aligned with purpose.

Finally, reflecting on the journey from human to hybrid attention, it is clear that we are not merely adding AI into organizations; we are fundamentally reshaping organizational sensemaking. When done thoughtfully, the introduction of AI attention mechanisms leads to organizations that can learn and decide more intelligently. They become more sensitive to their environments and more adept at responding, all while upholding the critical role of human insight and moral agency. This synthesis and outlook chapter has framed hybrid attention as an organizational capability that can be developed and honed. Much like organizations in the past learned to cultivate capabilities in quality management or innovation, organizations today and tomorrow will need to cultivate the capability for hybrid attention. This involves technology, yes, but also people, structures, and cultures co-evolving. It is a challenging task, but the payoff is an organization that is cognitively enriched, one that effectively "sees" and "thinks" with both human and machine eyes. As we conclude, we envision a future of work where human creativity and judgment are amplified by AI, not sidelined. The way forward is to ensure that our pursuit of machine intelligence remains grounded in the goal of augmenting human intelligence. In doing so, we align technological progress with humanistic values, steering away from mere automation and toward a richer paradigm of hybrid human–AI sensemaking. This paradigm holds the promise of organizations that are not only more efficient or data-driven, but ultimately more *intelligent, humane, and resilient* in the face of complexity.

References

Laine, J., Minkkinen, M., & Mäntymäki, M. (2024). Ethics-based AI auditing: A systematic literature review on conceptualizations of ethical principles and knowledge contributions to stakeholders. *Information & Management, 61*(5), 103969.

Ocasio, W. (1997). Towards an attention-based view of the firm. *Strategic Management Journal, 18*(S1), 187–206. https://doi.org/10.1002/(SICI)1097-0266(199707)18:1+

Papagiannidis, E., Enholm, I. M., Dremel, C., Mikalef, P., & Krogstie, J. (2023). Toward AI governance: Identifying best practices and potential barriers and outcomes. *Information Systems Frontiers, 25*(1), 123–141.

Schneider, J., Abraham, R., Meske, C., & Vom Brocke, J. (2023). Artificial intelligence governance for businesses. *Information Systems Management, 40*(3), 229–249.

Index

I. Ramos et al. (eds.), *Hybrid Attention in Organizations*, SpringerBriefs in Information Systems, https://doi.org/10.1007/978-3-032-30186-4

B

T

GPSR Compliance
The European Union's (EU) General Product Safety Regulation (GPSR) is a set of rules that requires consumer products to be safe and our obligations to ensure this.

If you have any concerns about our products, you can contact us on

ProductSafety@springernature.com

In case Publisher is established outside the EU, the EU authorized representative is:

Springer Nature Customer Service Center GmbH
Europaplatz 3
69115 Heidelberg, Germany

www.ingramcontent.com/pod-product-compliance
Ingram Content Group UK Ltd.
Pitfield, Milton Keynes, MK11 3LW, UK
UKHW051923030926
475117UK00001B/64
* 9 7 8 3 0 3 2 3 0 1 8 5 7 *